Academic Writing

A Handbook for International Students
Second edition

Stephen Bailey

Routledge
Taylor & Francis Group

LONDON AND NEW YORK

First edition published in 2003 by Nelson Thornes Ltd

This edition published 2006 by Routledge
2 Park Square, Milton Park, Abingdon, Oxon OX14 4RN

Simultaneously published in the USA and Canada
by Routledge
270 Madison Ave, New York, NY 10016

Reprinted 2006 (twice), 2007 (twice), 2008 (twice), 2009

Routledge is an imprint of the Taylor & Francis Group, an informa business

Typeset in Square, Swiss and Zapf Calligrafic by
Prepress Projects Ltd, Perth

Printed and bound in Great Britain by the MPG Books Group

British Library Cataloguing in Publication Data
A catalogue record for this book is available from the British Library

Library of Congress Cataloging in Publication Data
A catalog record has been requested for this book

ISBN10: 0-415-38419-2 (hbk)
ISBN10: 0-415-38420-6 (pbk)
ISBN13: 9-78-0-415-38419-3 (hbk)
ISBN13: 9-78-0-415-38420-9 (pbk)

Contents

Introduction

Academic Writing is for international students studying in colleges and universities where courses are taught in English. Those students who are not native speakers of English often find the written demands of their courses very challenging. In addition to learning academic English they need to adopt new conventions of style, referencing and layout.

Students usually have to complete a variety of writing tasks during their studies, ranging from short IELTS essays to lengthy dissertations. This writing may be done either under exam pressure or as coursework. In addition, the type of writing they are asked to do depends on the subject they are studying: future lawyers will be given quite different tasks from potential pharmacists.

Academic Writing recognises this variety of needs. It is a flexible course that allows students of all subjects and levels, from foundation to PhD, to practise those aspects of writing which are most important for their studies. The book is organised to provide maximum hands-on practice for students. They can work either with a teacher or by themselves, since the structure of the book has been made as simple as possible to allow them to find what they want quickly.

Academic Writing is divided into four parts. In Parts 1 and 2 the focus is on key writing skills, while Parts 3 and 4 offer revision and reference. Parts 2 and 3 are organised alphabetically for easy access.

Part 1: **The Writing Process** guides students from the initial stage of understanding the essay title, through note-making and paraphrasing, to the organisation of the essay and finally proof-reading.

Part 2: **Elements of Writing** deals with the skills that are needed for most types of assignment, such as making comparisons, giving examples and describing graphs.

Part 3: **Accuracy in Writing** gives remedial practice in those areas that students often find confusing, such as using articles, passives or prepositions.

Part 4: **Writing Models** offers examples of the types of writing that students commonly need, including letters and survey reports as well as essays.

There is also a **Writing Tests** section for checking progress.

The four parts are divided into sixty-one short units which teach practical writing skills and revise common difficulties. Each unit contains exercises, and a comprehensive answer key is given at the end. A system of cross-referencing helps students link related units together.

Although every effort has been made to make *Academic Writing* as clear and accurate as possible, I would welcome comment or criticism from either teachers or students.

Stephen Bailey
academicwriting@beeb.net

Instructions to students are printed like this:

Complete sentences with suitable words from the box below.

Cross-references in margins look like this:

cross-reference

2.11   *References and Quotations*

This means: refer to the unit on references and quotations in Part 2 (Unit 11)

Acknowledgements

I would like to thank the many staff and students at the Centre for English Language Education (CELE) at The University of Nottingham who have piloted these materials, and in particular my colleagues Ann Smith, Janet Sanders, John Rabone and Sandra Haywood for their help in unravelling some of the finer points of academic language.

My wife, Rene, deserves my warmest thanks for her unfailing support, advice and encouragement during the project's development.

The authors and publishers wish to thank the following for permission to reproduce photographs and other copyright material in this book.

Corel 76 (NT) p. 39; Corel 102 (NT) p. 128; Corel 392 (NT) p. 159; Corel 631 (NT) p. 44; Corel 787 (NT) p. 54; Joe Cornish/Digital Vision LL (NT) p. 50; Illustrated London News V1 (NT) p. 74; Illustrated London News V2 (NT) p. 4; Photodisc 31 (NT) p. 108; Photodisc 41 (NT) p. 61; Photodisc 46 (NT) pp. 74, 111; Photodisc 71 (NT) p. 12; Photodisc 72 (NT) p. 24; Stockbyte 31 (NT) p. 79.

Every effort has been made to contact copyright holders and the publishers apologise to anyone whose rights have been inadvertently overlooked and will be happy to rectify any errors or omissions.

Teachers and lecturers using this book with a class will be able to find extra teaching material within the teacher resources section of the Routledge website at http://www.routledge.com/education.

1. The Writing Process

Student Introduction

Most academic courses in English-medium colleges and universities use essays or other written tasks to assess students' work. These can be done as coursework, when a deadline of one or two months may be given, or in exams, when an essay often has to be finished in an hour.

The process of writing essays for coursework can be shown as a flowchart:

Understand essay title/requirements

Assess reading texts – choose most suitable

Select relevant areas of texts – keep record for references

Make notes on relevant areas, using paraphrasing and summarising skills

Combine a variety of sources where necessary

Select suitable structure for essay – make plan

Organise and write main body

Organise and write introduction

Organise and write conclusion

Critically read and rewrite where necessary

Final proof-reading

Part 1, *The Writing Process*, examines each of these stages in turn. If students are concerned only with preparing for exam writing they could miss out the reading and note-making stages, but if they have enough time they should work through every unit, preferably in the order given, since each stage builds on the previous one.

Although it is essential to learn the basic writing process, at the same time it is useful to be aware of the elements that contribute to good academic writing. When writing an introduction, for example, it is helpful to know how to write a definition, and so students working on *Introductions* (unit 1.14) should use the cross-reference boxes to look at the unit on *Definitions* in unit 2.5.

1.1 Background to Writing

Most university and college students are assessed through the production of written assignments. Some of the terms used to describe different types of assignments can be confusing. In addition, students need to be clear about the basic components of written texts. This unit provides an introduction to these topics.

1. Below are the most common types of written work produced or used by students.

   Complete the table to show the main purpose of each, and their usual approximate length.

Type	Purpose	Length
letter	for formal and informal communication	usually fewer than 500 words
notes		
report		
project		
essay		
thesis/dissertation		
article/paper		

2. Organisation of texts.

   a) *Explain the following terms in italics:*

      Shorter texts, e.g. essays, are normally organised:

      Introduction > Main Body > Conclusion

      Longer texts, e.g. dissertations and articles, may include (depending on subject area):

      Abstract > Contents > Introduction > Main Body > Case Study > Discussion > Findings > Conclusion > Acknowledgements > Bibliography/References > Appendices

      Books may also contain:

      Dedication > Foreword > Preface > Index

   b) *Match the definitions below to one of the terms in (2a).*

      i) Short summary (100–200 words) of the writer's purpose and findings   (......)

      ii) Section where various people who assisted the writer are thanked   (......)

iii) Final part where extra data, too detailed for
      the main text, are stored   (......)

iv)   List of all the books that the writer has
      consulted   (......)

v)   Section looking at a particular example, relevant
      to the main topic   (......)

vi)   Introductory part of the book which may give the
      writer's motives   (......)

vii) Alphabetical list of all topics in the text   (......)

cross-reference

3.1   Abbreviations
2.11   References and
       Quotations
3.14   Punctuation

3. Other text features

Abbreviations are often used to save space:

Call centres (CCs) feature prominently in the technology
mix . . .

Italics are used to show titles and words from other languages:

Where once the titles of *Armchair Theatre* and *The
Wednesday Play* celebrated . . .

Squatter housing (called *gecekondu* in Turkish) . . .

Footnotes are used to indicate references at the bottom of the
page:

In respect of Singapore the consensus is that the
government has made a difference.[3]

Endnotes are given to show references at the end of the article
or chapter:

The market for masonry construction may be divided into
housing and non-housing sectors [1].

Quotation marks are used to draw attention to a phrase, perhaps because it is being used in an unusual or new way:

> The research shows that the 'pains of imprisonment' for women are . . .

4. **All types of writing consist of a number of key elements.**

   Label the italic items in the text.

   a) . . . .   *THE ORIGINS OF THE INDUSTRIAL REVOLUTION*

   b) . . . .   *Introduction*

   c) . . . .   *It is generally agreed* that the Industrial Revolution began in Britain during the eighteenth century, with significant developments in the iron, steel and textile industries. But it is less clear what caused this sudden increase in production in key areas; different writers have examined the availability of capital, the growth of urban populations and the political

   d) . . . .   and religious climate. *All of these may have played a part, but first it is necessary to consider the precise nature of what is meant by 'industrial revolution'.*

   e) . . . .   *Industry had existed for thousands of years prior to the eighteenth century, but before this time society as a whole remained agricultural. With the arrival of the ironworks and cotton mills whole towns were dominated by industrial activity. At the same time, agriculture itself went through significant changes which produced more food for the growing urban population.*

cross-reference

1.12   *Organising Paragraphs*

5. **Why are all texts divided into paragraphs? How long are paragraphs?**

   Read the following text, from the introduction to an essay, and divide it into a suitable number of paragraphs.

   INVESTMENT

   Most people want to invest for the future, to cover unexpected financial difficulties and provide them with security. Different people, however, tend to have different requirements, so that a 25-year-old just leaving university would be investing for the long term, whereas a 60-year-old who had just retired would probably invest for income. Despite these differences, certain principles apply in most cases. The first issue to consider is

risk. In general, the greater the degree of risk in investment, the higher the return. Shares, for example, which can quickly rise or fall in value, typically have a higher yield than bonds, which offer good security but only pay about 5%. Therefore all investors must decide how much risk is appropriate in their particular situation. Diversification must also be considered in an investment strategy. Wise investors usually seek to spread their investments across a variety of geographical and business sectors. As accurate predictions of the future are almost impossible, it is best to have as many options as possible. A further consideration is investor involvement. Some investors opt for a high degree of involvement and want to buy and sell regularly, constantly watching the markets. Others want to invest and then forget about it. Personal involvement can be time-consuming and worrying, and many prefer to leave the management of their portfolios to professional fund managers.

1.2 Avoiding Plagiarism

All students have to face the issue of plagiarism. Plagiarism means taking information or ideas from another writer and using them in your own work, without acknowledging the source in an accepted manner. In academic work plagiarism can be a serious offence. This unit outlines the situation, but to fully avoid plagiarism students need to master the skills practised in units 1.6–1.10.

cross-reference	
2.11	*References and Quotations*
3.22	*Verbs of Reference*

1. *Which of the following would be considered as plagiarism?*

   a) Not providing a reference when you have used somebody's idea.

   b) Copying a few sentences from an article on the internet without giving a reference.

   c) Not giving a reference when you use commonly accepted ideas, e.g. Aids is a growing problem.

   d) Giving the reference but not using quotation marks when you take a sentence from another writer's article.

   e) Taking a paragraph from a classmate's essay without giving a reference.

   f) Presenting the results of your own research.

2. **To avoid plagiarism, and also to save having lengthy quotations in your work, it is necessary to paraphrase and summarise the original. Instead of this, students sometimes hope that changing a few words of the original will avoid charges of plagiarism. Clearly, you are not expected to alter every word of the original text, but your summary must be substantially different from the original.**

   Read the following extract on twentieth-century educational developments from Age of Extremes *by E. Hobsbawm:*

   > Almost as dramatic as the decline and fall of the peasantry, and much more universal, was the rise of the occupations which required secondary and higher education. Universal primary education, i.e. basic literacy, was indeed the aspiration of virtually all governments, so much so that by the late 1980s only the most honest or helpless states admitted to having as many as half their population illiterate, and only ten – all but Afghanistan in Africa – were prepared to concede that less than 20% of their population could read or write. (Hobsbawm, 1994, p. 295)

   Which of the following are plagiarised and which are acceptable?

   a) Almost as dramatic as the decline and fall of the peasantry, and much more general, was the rise of the professions which required secondary and higher education. Primary education for all, i.e. basic literacy, was indeed the aspiration of almost all governments, so much so that by the late 1980s only the most honest countries confessed to having as many as half their population illiterate, and only ten – all but Afghanistan in Africa – were prepared to admit that less than 20% of their population could read or write. (Hobsbawm, 1994, p. 295)

b) Nearly as dramatic as the decline of the peasantry was the rise of professions which required secondary and higher education. Primary education for everyone (basic literacy) was the aspiration of nearly all governments, so that by the late 1980s only the very honest countries confessed to having as many as half their population illiterate. Only ten (African) countries conceded that less than 20% of their population were literate. (Hobsbawm, 1994, p. 295)

c) As Hobsbawm (1994) argues, there was a marked increase in jobs needing secondary or higher education during the twentieth century. All but a few nations claimed that the majority of their people were literate. Universal primary education i.e. basic literacy was indeed the aspiration of virtually all governments. (p. 295)

d) There was a sharp and widespread increase in occupations requiring education above primary level. All governments set out to provide basic education, essentially literacy, for their people. By the end of the 1980s very few states would admit that the majority of their population were unable to read. (Hobsbawm, 1994, p. 295)

3. *What makes the difference between plagiarised and acceptable work? List your ideas below.*

Acceptable	Plagiarised
Some vocabulary kept from original	

1.3 From Titles to Outlines

Most written work begins with a title, and students must be quite clear what question the title is asking before starting to plan the essay and read around the topic. This unit deals with analysing titles and making basic essay outlines.

1. When preparing to write an essay, it is essential to identify the main requirements of the title. You must be clear about what areas your teacher wants you to cover. These will then determine the organisation of the essay. For example:

    The state should play no part in the organisation of industry – discuss.

    Here the key word is *discuss*. Discussing involves examining the benefits and drawbacks of something.

    Underline the key words in the following titles and consider what they are asking you to do.

    a) Define information technology (IT) and outline its main applications in medicine.

    b) Compare and contrast the appeal process in the legal systems of Britain and the USA.

    c) Evaluate the effect of mergers in the motor industry in the last ten years.

    d) Trace the development of primary education in one country. Illustrate some of the issues currently facing this sector.

    Note that most of the titles above have *two* terms in the title. You must decide how much importance to give to each section of the essay: e.g. title (a) might require 10% for the definition and 90% for the explanation.

2. The following terms are also commonly used in essay titles.

    Match the terms to the definitions on the right.

Analyse	Give a clear and simple account
Describe	Make a proposal and support it
Examine	Deal with a complex subject by giving the main points
State	Divide into sections and discuss each critically
Suggest	Give a detailed account
Summarise	Look at the various parts and their relationships

1.11   Planning Essays

3. **Almost all essays, reports and articles have the same basic pattern of organisation:**

Introduction
Main body
Conclusion

The structure of the main body depends on what the title is asking you to do. In the case of a 'discuss' type essay, the main body is often divided into two parts, one looking at the advantages of the topic and the other looking at the disadvantages.

An outline for the example in (1) might look like this:

The state should play no part in the organisation of industry – discuss.

Introduction	various economic theories: Marxist, Keynesian, free market
	most economies display trend towards privatisation
Disadvantages	state protects workers from exploitation, e.g. children
	consumers protected from dangerous products, e.g. medical drugs
	state has resources to support new technologies
Advantages	few state-controlled economies are successful, e.g. Soviet Union
	state control does not encourage individual effort
	state intervention often leads to corruption
Conclusion	state has a role in protecting weakest, but should not interfere with free enterprise

4. *Write an outline for one of the other titles in (1).*

Title	
Introduction	
Main body	
Conclusion	

5. **Teachers often complain that students write essays which do not answer the question set.**

    Consider the following titles and decide which sections should be included in each essay.

a) Describe the growth of the European Union since 1975 and suggest its likely form by 2020.

    A short account of European history 1900–2000

    An analysis of candidates for membership before 2020

    A discussion of the current economic situation in Europe

    A summary of the enlargement of the EU from 1975 to now

b) Summarise the arguments in favour of privatisation and evaluate its record in Britain.

    A case study of electricity privatisation

    An analysis of the international trends in privatisation

    A study of major privatisations in the UK

    A discussion of the benefits achieved by privatisation

c) To what extent is tuberculosis (TB) a disease of poverty?

    A definition of TB

    A report on the spread of TB worldwide

    A case study showing how TB relates to social class

    A discussion of new methods of treating the disease

d) Nursery education is better for children than staying at home with mother – discuss.

A study of the growth of nurseries in the UK since 1995

A report on the development of children who remain at home until age 5

A discussion comparing speaking ability in both groups of children

An analysis of the increase of women in the labour market since 1960

e) Compare studying in a library with using the internet. Will the former become redundant?

The benefits of using books

The drawbacks of internet sources

Predicted IT developments in the next 15 years

The developments in library services since 1970

6. *Underline the key terms in the following titles, and decide what you are being asked to do.*

Example:

<u>Relate</u> the development of railways to the rise of nineteenth-century European nationalism.

Relate means to link one thing to another. The title is asking for links to be made between the growth of railways in Europe in the nineteenth century and the political philosophy of nationalism. The writer must decide if there was a connection or not.

a) Identify the main causes of rural poverty in China.

b) Calculate the likely change in coffee consumption that would result from a 10% fall in the price of coffee beans.

c) Classify the desert regions of Asia and suggest possible approaches to halting their spread.

1.4　Evaluating Texts

Having understood the title and made an outline, the next step is probably to read around the subject. Although a reading list may be given, it is still vital to be able to assess the usefulness of journal articles and books. Time spent learning these skills will be repaid by avoiding the use of unreliable or irrelevant materials.

1. When reading a text, it is important to ask yourself questions about the value of the text. Is this text fact or opinion? If fact, is it true? If opinion, do I agree? Can this writer be trusted? These questions can be seen as a process:

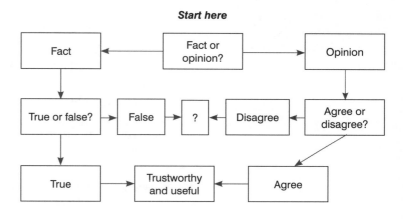

2. *Read the following sentences and decide first if they are fact or opinion. Then decide if you agree with the opinions, and if the factual sentences are true.*

	Opinion or fact?	Agree or disagree?	True or false?
Example: *The USA has the biggest economy in the world*	*Fact*		*True*
a) Shakespeare was a great writer			
b) Shakespeare wrote textbooks			
c) Smoking can be dangerous			
d) Too many people smoke in Britain			
e) 95% of criminals cannot read			
f) Poor education causes half of all crime			

3. **It can be seen that even short sentences, such as (2f) above, can contain a mixture of fact and opinion. Most longer texts, of course, consist of both.**

    Read the following text about crime in Britain and underline facts (_____) and opinions (. . . . .).

    a) Britain has one of the highest crime rates in the world.

    b) A robbery takes place every five seconds. Clearly, criminals are not afraid of the police.

    c) Even if they are caught, few criminals ever appear in court.

    d) Most of those who are found guilty are let off with a small fine.

    e) To reduce crime, we need more police and tougher punishments.

4. **The text can be evaluated as follows:**

    a) Fact, but only partly true. Britain does not have one of the highest overall crime rates in the world. For some crimes, e.g. car crime, the rate is high, but other countries, e.g. South Africa, have much higher rates of violent crime.

    b) This may or may not be true, but it does not follow that criminals are unafraid of the police.

    c) Fact, but not true. A significant number of those arrested are charged and later prosecuted.

    d) This fact is distorted. A fine is not 'letting off'. What is meant by 'small'?

    e) This is opinion. More police would probably help reduce crime, but it is not clear if more severe punishments would have that result.

    From this it can be seen that, even if the facts are correct, the opinions that are expressed may not be reliable. The evaluation above would suggest that the writer of the original text could not be trusted, and it would be better to look for another source.

5. *Evaluate the following texts in a similar way, using the table below. First underline and assess the facts and opinions, then decide if the text as a whole is trustworthy.*

Text	Are the facts true?	Do I agree with the opinions?	Trustworthy?
a			
b			
c			
d			

a) Every year large numbers of students travel abroad to study at university. Most of them spend thousands of pounds on their degree courses. The cost of travel and accommodation adds significantly to their expenses. But they could save a lot of money by studying their courses on-line, using the internet and email. Increasing numbers of universities are offering tuition by the internet, and this has many advantages for students. In the future most students are likely to stay at home and study in front of a computer.

b) London is an ideal city for young students. Britain's lively capital, with a population of two million, is the perfect place to live and study. Cheap, comfortable accommodation is always available, and transport is provided by the clean and reliable underground railway system. Another advantage is the friendly citizens, who are well-known for their custom of stopping to chat with strangers. Overall, London is probably the best place in the world to study English.

c) Global warming affects most people in the world, especially those living in low-lying areas near the sea. It has been predicted that the melting of polar ice may cause the sea to rise by as much as twelve metres by 2050. This would cause flooding in many major coastal cities, such as Tokyo. It has been suggested that the best solution to this problem may be for mankind to become amphibious, like frogs. It is argued that life was originally found in the sea, and so it would merely be a return to our original habitat.

d) There is significant new evidence of the effects of heavy alcohol consumption by young people. In Britain in 2000 nearly 800 people under 44 died from cirrhosis of the liver, a condition which is mainly caused by excess drinking. This is over four times higher than the number in 1970. The growing problem seems to be due to 'binge' drinking among the young, when drinkers deliberately set out to get drunk. As a result, the government is studying the possibility of compulsory health warnings on alcohol advertising.

1.5 Understanding Purpose and Register

Having decided that a text is reliable, a student must read and understand as much as necessary for the needs of the essay. Understanding a text is not just a matter of vocabulary; the reader needs to find out the writer's intentions. Is the writer aiming to inform, persuade, describe or entertain? In addition the reader should be clear about the type of English the writer is using: how formal is the tone? The answer to these questions may affect the way a student uses the material.

PURPOSE

1. *Compare the two extracts below:*

   a) Rebus College is seeking candidates for the position of Treasurer. As the Chief Financial Officer of the College, the Treasurer is responsible for working with the senior administration and Trustees to develop and implement a financial strategic vision for the College.

   b) Are you wondering what to do with that jumper you were given for Christmas that's two sizes too small – or, worse, the personal stereo that simply doesn't work? Well, don't worry. Chances are, you'll be able to get your dud gifts swapped, fixed or get a refund. And, armed with our guide to your rights, you'll be able to get any defective products sorted.

The first extract is written to **inform** the reader about a job vacancy and to give information about the work. The second aims to **persuade** the reader to buy the guide described. The language style, or register, of the extracts is also very different. The first uses very formal vocabulary such as *seeking*, *position* and *implement*. The second uses an informal tone, the pronoun *you*, the question form and informal vocabulary such as *dud* and *swapped*.

2. *Read the following extracts and complete the table using one or two of the following: inform/amuse/persuade/entertain.*

Text	Purpose
a	
b	
c	

   a) The lower you are in the office hierarchy, the more disgusting your sandwiches. You can safely assume that a chicken and banana man is not a main board director. Some people, generally those in accounts, have had the same sandwich for the past 30 years. People like to prove how busy they are by eating their sandwich at their desk. But this is counter-productive, because every time you take a mouthful the phone rings, and you'll only get to finish that last mouthful just before you go home.

b) Writing for publication can be both profitable and enjoyable. It's open to everyone, because you don't need any qualifications. In Britain there is a huge demand for new materials, with thousands of newspapers and magazines published every week. In addition there are TV and radio programmes, the theatre and films. Given this situation, there are many openings for new writers. But the director of one of the UK's main writing colleges, the Writing Academy, advises: 'to enter this market successfully you must have good training'.

c) The Advertising Standards Authority makes sure that advertising is legal, decent, honest and truthful. The Authority safeguards the public by ensuring that the rules contained in the British Code of Advertising Practice are followed by everyone who prepares and publishes advertisements in the UK, and that advice is freely available to prevent problems arising. The Code lays down what is and is not acceptable in advertisements, except for those on TV and radio.

cross-reference

2.13   Style
3.18   Verbs – Formality

REGISTER

3. **What are the differences between the following types of English? Where might each one be found?**

Academic	Jargon
Archaic	Journalistic
Formal	Literary

4. *Match the examples below with the types of English listed above:*

a) Demographic data are given in Table 1. Twenty-three men and thirty-two women were available for follow-up examination. The sex and age distributions were approximately the same as in the total original baseline group.

b) The services, information or data (collectively, "information") made available at the company web site are provided "as is", without warranties of any kind. The Company expressly disclaims any representations and warranties, including without limitation, the implied warranties of merchantability and fitness for particular purpose.

c) The Creative Labs Inspire 6.1 6600 speaker set matches up well with the Sound Blaster Audigy 2 sound card, which has support for 24 bit processing and surround sound. The speaker set consists of five satellites, a centre speaker and a subwoofer.

d) Alexandria Main Station: midnight. A deathly heavy dew. The noise of wheels cracking the slime-slithering pavements. Yellow pools of phosphorous light, and corridors of darkness like tears in the dull brick façade of a stage set. Policemen in the shadows.

e) Nottingham, notwithstanding the navigation of the Trent, is not esteemed a town of very great trade, other than is usual to inland towns; the chief manufacture carried on here is frame-work knitting for stockings, the same as at Leicester, and some glass, and earthen ware-houses; the latter much increased since the increase of tea-drinking . . .

f) When Mary Graham went into hospital to have a new knee, she discovered a computer would be playing a big part in the operation. In the past, surgeons have relied on the naked eye to ensure they've got a replacement joint in the right position. But now they will be able to achieve almost total accuracy using a computer to guide them through the operation.

5. **The following terms are used to describe special features in written English.**

   Match them with the examples (in italics) below.

Idiom*	Euphemism*
Metaphor	Proverb*
Paradox	Hyperbole*
Analogy	Irony*

   a) The king *passed away* on August 3rd 1879.

   b) She claimed that further research was *the key* to solving the problem.

   c) As the Chinese say, *the longest journey begins with a single step*.

  d) She felt that *the older she got, the less she really knew*.

  e) The negotiation process reminded him of *a game of chess*.

  f) By the end of the semester most students were *in the red*.

  g) When a student arrived late, the teacher asked *if he had had a good sleep*.

  h) He claimed that his book was *the most important work of the century*.

6. When writing academic work, it is important not to use phrases met in non-academic texts, e.g. newspapers or magazines. The features marked with an asterisk (*) above should be avoided in academic writing.

   Find examples of them in the sentences below and rewrite them in more academic style.

   a) Obesity is the most serious problem facing civilisation today.

   b) One cause is the famously healthy Western diet of chocolate and hamburgers.

   c) So people with podgy tummies should think about fighting the flab.

   d) They should pull themselves together, and get down to the gym.

   e) They must remember the saying: God helps those who help themselves.

1.6   Selecting Key Points

After selecting and understanding the most relevant texts, the next step is usually to make notes on the sections of the texts that relate to your topic. Units 1.6–1.9 practise this process, which involves a number of inter-linked skills. This unit deals with the identification of relevant information and ideas.

cross-reference

1.7   Note-making

1. **The first stage of note-making is to identify the key points in the text for your purpose. You are preparing to write an essay on 'Changing patterns of longevity'.**

   Study the following example (key points in italics).

   ### WHY WOMEN LIVE LONGER

   Despite the overall increase in life expectancy *in Britain* over the past century, *women still live significantly longer than men*. In fact, in 1900 men could expect to live to 49 and women to 52, a difference of three years, while *now the figures are 74 and 79*, which shows that the gap has increased to five years.

   Various reasons have been suggested for this situation, such as the possibility that men may die earlier because they take more risks. But a team of British *scientists have recently found a likely answer in the immune system*, which protects the body from diseases. *The thymus is the organ which produces the T cells* which actually combat illnesses. Although both sexes suffer from deterioration of the thymus as they age, *women appear to have more T cells in their bodies than men of the same age*. It is this, the scientists believe, that *gives women better protection* from potentially fatal diseases such as influenza and pneumonia.

   Having selected these sections of the text, you can then go on to make notes from them:

   > British women live longer than men: 79/ 74 years
   >
   > reasons? new research suggests immune system/thymus > T cells
   >
   > women have more T cells than men = better protection

2. *Read the following and then choose a suitable title which expresses the key point.*

   Title:

   Dean Kamen is a 50-year-old American eccentric who is also a multi-millionaire. He always wears blue denim shirts and jeans, even when visiting his friend, the president, in the White House. He flies to work by helicopter, which he also uses for visiting his private island off the coast of Connecticut. As an undergraduate Kamen developed the first pump that would give regular doses of medicine to patients. The patent for this and other original medical inventions has produced a huge income, allowing him to run his own research company which, among many other projects, has produced the iBot, the world's first wheelchair which can climb stairs.

3.   *Underline three key points in the following text.*

EMPOWERING HEALTHCARE

In many parts of the world hospitals have none of the modern health equipment that is common in western countries. This is partly because it is expensive, but also because electricity supplies are often unreliable, while trained staff who can read the complex displays may not be available. Now, Freeplay Energy, the company which developed the wind-up radio, is planning to introduce a range of medical equipment which can be used in those areas. All the machines will be of simple, robust design which will either use solar power or foot pedals, making expensive battery replacement unnecessary. Prototypes are currently on trial in South African hospitals, where their performance can be compared with more sophisticated machines.

4.   *Underline the key points in the following text.*

THE SIXTH WAVE?

Lord May, the president of the Royal Society, has claimed that the world is facing a wave of extinctions similar to the five mass extinctions of past ages. He calculates that the current rate of extinction is between 100 and 1,000 times faster than the historical average. The cause of previous extinctions, such as the one which killed the dinosaurs, is uncertain, but was probably an external event such as collision with a comet.

However, the present situation is caused by human consumption of plants, which has resulted in a steady increase in agriculture and a consequent reduction in habitat for animals. Although many people are still hungry, food production has increased by 100% since 1965.

Lord May also pointed out that it was very difficult to make accurate estimates as nobody knew how many species of animals lived on the planet. So far 1.5 million species had been named, but the true figure might be as high as 100 million. Our ignorance of this made it almost impossible to work out the actual rate of extinction. However, the use of intelligent guesses suggests that losses over the past century were comparable with the extinctions of earlier periods, evidence of which is found in the fossil record.

5.   **When preparing to write an essay you may be concerned with only one aspect of a text, so that your key points relate only to the topic you are examining.**

a)   *You are planning to write an essay on 'Marketing – art or science?' Read the text below and underline the sections relevant to your essay.*

BOTTLED WATER UNDER ATTACK

The Water Companies Association (WCA) has claimed that bottled water costs 700 times more than tap water, but is often of inferior quality. The chief executive of the WCA pointed out that although bottled water advertising often associated the product with sport and health there was no truth in this link. The reality, she said, was that the packaging of bottled water was environmentally damaging, since millions of empty bottles had to be disposed of in rubbish tips. 2% of samples of bottled water failed a purity test conducted by the Drinking Water Inspectorate, while only 0.3% of tap water samples failed the same test. Labels on bottled water often referred to 'spring' and 'natural water', which were meaningless phrases. In addition, bottled water was imported from as far as Korea and Kenya, which was a waste of resources. These criticisms, however, were rejected by the British Soft Drinks Association, which argued that bottled water was a successful business founded on giving the customers choice, quality and convenience.

b)   *You are preparing an essay on 'The application of DNA research to the development of vaccines'. Read the text and underline the relevant sections.*

NEW LIGHT ON THE PLAGUE

The plague, which first struck Europe in the sixth century, was one of the great disasters of history. In the fourteenth century it became the Black Death, when it may have killed one-third of the entire population. The microbe that causes the disease lives on rats, and is passed on to humans by the bite of a flea. It still survives today, though outbreaks are less deadly: the World Health Organization receives reports of 3,000 cases annually. Scientists believe that the microbe was originally a stomach infection, but evolved into a more lethal disease about 1,500 years ago.

Now the genetic code of the plague bacterium has been 'read' by scientists; a total of 465 million 'letters' of DNA. They believe that this will help in the development of

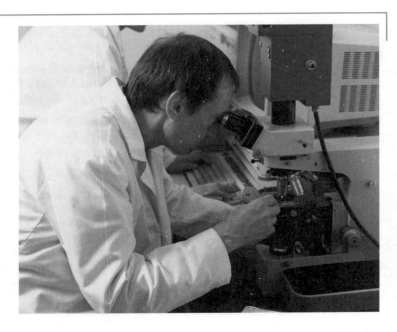

vaccines for the plague, one of which has begun clinical trials. In parts of Africa drug-resistant strains of the disease have evolved, which gives added importance to the work, as does the threat that the plague might be used as an agent of bacteriological warfare.

1.7　Note-making

Effective note-making is a key writing skill, with a number of practical uses. Good note-making techniques lead to accurate essays. Although you are the only person who will read your notes, clarity and organisation are important to save time and errors at the writing stage.

1.2　*Avoiding Plagiarism*

1. What are the main reasons for note-taking?

Add to the ideas below.

a)　to avoid plagiarism

b)

c)

d)

cross-reference

1.6　*Selecting Key Points*

2. Effective note-making is part of a sequence.

What comes before and after?

Note-making

3. *You are writing an essay on 'Computer security'. You find the following extract from an article in a magazine called* **Computing Tomorrow,** *volume 15 (2005), on pages 134–7. The author is Y. Lee. Read the text and complete the notes.*

PICTURE PASSWORDS?

In computing, passwords are commonly used to limit access to official users. Yet the widespread use of passwords has serious drawbacks. Office workers now have to remember an average of twelve system passwords. In theory they should use different passwords for each site, but in reality these would be impossible to remember, so many people use the same password for all. An additional problem is that the majority use simple words such as hello, or names of family members, instead of more secure combinations of numbers and letters, such as 6ANV76Y. This permits computer hackers to download dictionaries, which will quickly find the word and allow them access.

When system users forget their passwords there is extra expense in supplying new ones, while if people are forced to change passwords frequently they often write them down, making systems even less secure. Therefore, it is clear that the idea of passwords, which have been used as security devices for thousands of years, may need rethinking.

One possible alternative has been developed by the American firm Real User, and is called Passfaces. In order to access the system a worker has to select a series of photographs of faces from a randomly generated sequence. If the pictures are selected in the correct order access is granted. This concept depends on the human ability to recognise and remember a huge number of different faces, and the advantage is that such a sequence cannot be told to anyone or written down, so is more secure. It is claimed that the picture sequence, which uses photographs of university students, is easier to remember than passwords, and it has now been adopted for the United States Senate.

Source: Lee, Y. (2005) *Computing Tomorrow* **15** pp.134–137.

Computer passwords

– generally used to protect sites from hackers

Drawbacks

a) office workers must remember av. 12 passwords → most use same one

b)

c)

d)

_____

a)

b)

c)

d)

---

cross-reference

2.11   *References and Quotations*

3.1   *Abbreviations*

4.   **Effective note-making**

employs

- Headings, sub-headings, underlining and listing to organise the data clearly

- Simplified grammar (few articles, pronouns or prepositions)

- Symbols (such as = or +) and abbreviations (pp. or av.)

NB

a)   Do not abbreviate too much, or you may find the notes impossible to understand in the future.

b) Sources should be noted in the same format as they will appear in your references.

c) You need to develop your own style for note-making, to suit the nature of your subject.

5. *You have been told to write an essay on 'Malaria – can it be controlled?' You decide to make notes on the following article from a magazine called* **Medical Report** *(Volume 34 1998, pp. 78–86). The author's name is Irene Nemecova. Make notes on the whole text in the box below.*

MALARIA FIGHTS BACK

Drug-resistant strains of malaria, already one of the world's major killers, are steadily spreading across the globe. The deadly strains have established themselves in South-East Asia and South America, and have recently begun to spread across India and Africa. Formerly under control in many areas, the disease now threatens two billion people living in more than 100 countries. Estimates suggest that there are now more than 350 million cases of malaria a year – a total four times the level of the early 1970s. In Africa alone the disease kills one million children each year.

Several factors are responsible for this disturbing development. Spreading world poverty has deprived nations of funds for sanitation, so that many health projects have been stopped, while increased movements of migrant workers and tourists have carried infections more rapidly from one country to another. At the same time, the overuse of drugs, especially antibiotics, has led to the establishment of resistant strains of diseases.

As well as this, hopes that genetic engineers might soon develop the world's first malaria vaccine, a long-sought goal, have been questioned recently by several scientists. 'There are so many strains of malaria parasite,' said one scientist, 'and each is able to alter its chemical surface and trick its way past the body's defences. We'd need a remarkable vaccine to cope with that. However, a malaria vaccine is now undergoing human trials and may be available for use if proved successful.'

6. *You are preparing to write an essay on 'The impact of climate on history'. The text below is taken from page 221 of a book called* **Volcanic Disasters** *by E. B. Pitnam, published in 1993. Underline the relevant points and make notes.*

One of the greatest explosions in modern history occurred in 1815, when an Indonesian volcano called Mt. Tambora blew up. The eruption involved about 100 cubic kilometres of material being blown into the sky, with huge loss of life both on land and sea. Large quantities of volcanic dust were ejected into the atmosphere, and this dust gradually spread around the world, causing alarming events on the other side of the world.

In New England in north-eastern USA farmers were hit by bitterly cold weather in June and July 1816. Much of the harvest was lost due to repeated waves of frost and snow in the middle of summer. The same pattern was recorded in Europe, where agriculture was still suffering the effects of the Napoleonic Wars. In France wheat prices reached their highest point of the century in 1817.

As European demand for food rose, prices doubled in America. Although some profited from the shortages, others were driven to emigrate into the unexplored lands to the west. Numbers leaving Vermont, for example, increased by 100% between 1816 and 1817.

1.8 Paraphrasing

Paraphrasing involves changing a text so that it is quite different from the source, while retaining the meaning. This skill is important in several areas of academic work, but this unit focuses on using paraphrasing in note-making and summary writing. Effective paraphrasing is vital in academic writing to avoid the risk of plagiarism.

1. **Although paraphrasing techniques are used in summary writing, paraphrasing does not aim to shorten the length of a text, merely to restate it.**

    For example:

    Evidence of a lost civilisation has been found off the coast of China

    could be paraphrased:

    Remains of an ancient society have been discovered in the sea near China

cross-reference

2.14   Synonyms
3.2   Academic Vocabulary

2. **A good paraphrase is significantly different from the wording of the original, without altering the meaning at all.**

    Read the text below and then decide which is the better paraphrase, (a) or (b).

    Ancient Egypt collapsed in about 2180 BC. Studies conducted of the mud from the River Nile showed that at this time the mountainous regions which feed the Nile suffered from a prolonged drought. This would have had a devastating effect on the ability of Egyptian society to feed itself.

    a) The sudden ending of Egyptian civilisation over 4,000 years ago was probably caused by changes in the weather in the region to the south. Without the regular river flooding there would not have been enough food.

    b) Research into deposits of the Egyptian Nile indicate that a long dry period in the mountains at the river's source may have led to a lack of water for irrigation around 2180 BC, which was when the collapse of Egyptian society began.

3. **Techniques**

    a) Changing vocabulary:

    studies > research   society > civilisation
    mud > deposits

    NB Not all words and phrases can be paraphrased. For example, *economics*, *socialism* or *global warming* have no effective synonyms.

b) Changing word class:

Egypt (n.) > Egyptian (adj.) mountainous regions (adj. + n.) > in the mountains (n.)

c) Changing word order:

Ancient Egypt collapsed > the collapse of Egyptian society began

4. *Find synonyms for the words in italics.*

a) The *growth* of the *car* industry *parallels* the *development* of *modern* capitalism.

Example:

The *rise* of the *automobile* industry *matches* the *progress* of *contemporary* capitalism.

b) It *began* in France and Germany, but *took off* in the United States.

c) There Henry Ford *adapted* the moving *production* line from the Chicago meat industry to *motor* manufacturing, *thus* inventing mass production.

5. *Change the word class of the words in italics, and then rewrite the sentences.*

a) In the 1920s Alfred Sloan's *management* theories *helped* General Motors to become the world's *dominant* car company.

Example:

In the 1920s, with *help* from the *managerial* theories of Alfred Sloan, General Motors *dominated* the world's car companies.

b) After the Second World War the industry *developed* 'planned obsolescence', whereby *frequent* model changes encouraged customers to buy new cars more often than they needed to.

c) Later, from the 1970s, *environmentalists* began to *criticise* the industry for *producing* inefficient models which used too much fuel, contributing to global warming.

6. *Change the word order of the following sentences (other changes may be needed).*

a) At this time, trades unions became increasingly militant in defence of their members' jobs.

Example:

At this time increasingly militant trades unions defended their members' jobs.

b) Today the industry owns some of the strongest brands in the world.

c) However, many major car companies struggle with stagnant markets and falling profits.

7. *Combine all these techniques to paraphrase the paragraph as fully as possible.*

FOUR WHEELS GOOD

The growth of the car industry parallels the development of modern capitalism. It began in France and Germany, but took off in the United States. There Henry Ford adapted the moving production line from the Chicago meat industry to motor manufacturing, thus inventing mass production. In the 1920s Alfred Sloan's management theories helped General Motors to become the world's dominant car company. After the Second World War the industry developed 'planned obsolescence', whereby frequent model changes encouraged customers to buy new cars more often than they needed to. Later, from the 1970s, environmentalists began to criticise the industry for producing inefficient models which used too much fuel, contributing to global warming. At this time, trades unions became increasingly militant in defence of their members' jobs. Today the industry owns some of the strongest brands in the world. However, many major car companies struggle with stagnant markets and falling profits.

8. *Use the same techniques to paraphrase the following text.*

Before the last century no humans had visited Antarctica, and even today the vast continent has a winter population of fewer than 200 people. However, a recent report from a New Zealand government agency outlines the scale of the pollution problem in the ice and snow. Although untouched compared with other regions in the world, the bitter cold of Antarctica means that the normal process of decay is prevented. As a result some research stations are surrounded by the rubbish of nearly 60 years' operations.

Despite popular belief, the polar continent is really a desert, with less precipitation than the Sahara. In the past, snowfall slowly covered the waste left behind, like beer cans or dead ponies, but now, possibly due to global warming, the ice is thinning and these are being exposed. Over 10 years ago the countries using Antarctica agreed a treaty on waste disposal, under which everything is to be taken home, and this is slowly improving the situation. However, the scientists do not want everything removed. The remains of very early expeditions at the beginning of the twentieth century have acquired historical value and will be preserved.

1.9 Summary Writing

Making summaries is a common activity in everyday life. If a friend asks you about a book you are reading, you do not tell her about everything in the book. Instead, you make a summary of the most interesting and important aspects. The same principle applies to summarising in academic work.

1. *Choose three of the topics below and write summaries in no more than twelve words each.*

   Example:

   Birmingham – Birmingham is a large industrial city in the English west midlands.

   a) Your home town

   b) Bill Gates

   c) Your academic subject

   d) The last book you read

   e) A film you saw recently

   Look at the summaries you have written above. What are the features of a successful summary?

2. **Summary writing is an important skill in academic work. Different kinds of summaries are needed in different situations.**

   List as many study uses for summary writing as you can think of.

   making notes from lectures

   . . . .

   . . . .

3. **In essay writing students often have to summarise part of a book or journal article.**

   The summary may be just one or two sentences, to explain the main idea of the article, and perhaps compare it with another summarised text, or it might be necessary to include much more detail. In other words, a summary can range from 1–2% of the original to more than 50%: summarising is a flexible tool.

   At first students need to follow a series of steps to summarise successfully. With practice the number of steps may be reduced, as the process becomes more automatic.

   Complete the list of stages in a successful summary by using phrases from the box.

i)	use your own words	ii) key points
iii)	important ideas	iv) order of ideas where necessary

a) Read the text carefully and check key vocabulary.

b) Underline or highlight the . . . .

c) Make notes of these, taking care to . . . .

d) Write the summary using the notes, re-organising the . . . .
. . . .

e) Check the summary to make sure no . . . .
. . . . . . have been omitted or distorted.

4. *Read the following text and compare the summaries. Decide which is best, giving reasons.*

Researchers in France and the United States have recently reported that baboons are able to think abstractly. It has been known for some time that chimpanzees are capable of abstract thought, but baboons are a more distant relation to mankind. In the experiment, scientists trained two baboons to use a personal computer and a joystick. The animals had to match computer designs which were basically the same, but had superficial differences. In the experiment the baboons performed better than would be expected by chance. The researchers describe their study in an article in the *Journal of Experimental Psychology.*

a) French and American scientists have shown for the first time that baboons have the ability to think in an abstract way. The animals were taught to use a computer, and then had to select patterns that were similar, which they did at a rate better than chance.

b) Baboons are a kind of monkey more distant from man than chimpanzees. Although it is known that chimpanzees are able to think abstractly, until recently it was not clear if baboons could do the same. But new research by various scientists has shown that this is so.

c) According to a recent article in the *Journal of Experimental Psychology*, baboons are able to think in an abstract way. The article describes how researchers trained two baboons to use a personal computer and a joystick. The animals did better than would be expected.

cross-reference

1.6   *Selecting Key Points*

5. *Read the following text and underline the key points.*

Indian researchers are trying to find out if there is any truth in old sayings which claim to predict the weather. In Gujarat farmers have the choice of planting either peanuts, which are more profitable in wet years, or castor, which does better in drier conditions. The difference depends on the timing of the monsoon rains, which can arrive at any time between the beginning and the middle of June. Farmers, however, have to decide what seeds to sow in April or May.

There is a local saying, at least a thousand years old, which claims that the monsoon starts 45 days after the flowering of a common tree, *Cassia fistula*. Dr Kanani, an agronomist from Gujarat Agricultural University, has been studying the relationship since 1996, and has found that the tree does successfully predict the approximate date of the monsoon's arrival.

6. *Complete the following notes of the key points.*

a) Indian scientists checking ancient . . . .
    . . . .

b) Old saying links monsoon to . . . .
    . . . .

c) Used by farmers to select peanuts (for wet) or . . . .
    . . . .

d) Dr Kanani of Gujarat Agricultural University has found
    that . . . .
    . . . .
    . . . .

cross-reference

3.7   *Conjunctions*

7. *Link the notes together to make a complete summary using conjunctions where necessary. Check the final text for factual accuracy.*

Indian scientists are checking

8. *The original text was about 150 words. The summary above uses about 50, so the original has been reduced by about 65%. However, it might be necessary to summarise still further. Using the same techniques, summarise the summary in about twenty words.*

9. *Summarise the following article in about 75 words.*

South Korea is planning to move its capital from Seoul to a new site in the middle of the country. Although Seoul has been the capital since the fourteenth century, the city of over 20 million is now very crowded, and also close to the hostile armies of North Korea. The new capital is planned to cost $45 billion, with construction finishing by 2012.

There is, however, strong opposition to the project, since similar schemes in other countries have taken far longer and cost much more than originally planned. Australia, for example, took over 70 years to finish building Canberra, while Nigeria has never completed its planned new capital, Abuja. Both Brazil and Malaysia have found that the building of new capitals (Brasilia and Putrajaya) can sharply increase the national burden of debt. Even if the government does eventually move to the new capital, it is unlikely that South Korea's main businesses will follow it, so Seoul will probably continue to be the country's principal city.

1.10 Combining Sources

Most essays require the writer to read more than one book or article. Your essay should include a summary of the views of the different sources you have studied. In some cases the contrast between the ideas of different writers may be the focus of the essay. This unit examines ways of presenting such varying views.

cross-reference

2.11   References and
       Quotations
3.22   Verbs of Reference

1. *Read the example, from a study of women's experience of prison.*

> *According to* Giallombardo (1966), women alleviated the pains of imprisonment by developing kinship links with other inmates. Similarly, Heffernan (1972) *found* that adaptation to prison was facilitated by the creation of a pseudo-family. Owen (1998) also *notes* that the female subculture is based on personal relationships with other women inmates. Others, however, *believe* that the subculture in women's prisons is undergoing a gradual shift that more closely resembles that of male prisons. Fox (1982) *states*, for example, that the cooperative caring prison community that has embodied characterizations of female prisons has evolved into a more dangerous and competitive climate.

   a)   How many writers are mentioned?

   b)   What is the function of the words in italics?

   c)   What phrase is used to mark the point in the text where there is a shift from one point of view to another?

2. **Below are two sources used for an essay titled 'Should genetically modified (GM) foods have a role in future agriculture?'**

   Read the sources first, then the essay extract.

   Source A

   Genetic modification (GM) is the most recent application of biotechnology to food, which can also be called genetic engineering or genetic manipulation. The phrase 'genetically modified organisms' or GMOs is used frequently in the scientific literature to describe plants and animals which have had DNA introduced into them by means other than the 'natural' process of an egg and a sperm.

   New species have always evolved through natural selection by means of random genetic variation. Early farmers used this natural variation to selectively breed wild animals, plants and even micro-organisms such as yogurt cultures and yeasts. They produced domesticated variants better suited to the needs of humans, long before the scientific basis for the process was understood. Despite this long history of careful improvement, such procedures are now labelled 'interfering with nature'.

Source B

Genetic modification (GM) is in fact far more than a mere development of selective breeding techniques. Combining genetic material from species that cannot breed naturally is an interference in areas which may be highly dangerous. The consequences of this kind of manipulation cannot be foreseen.

It seems undeniable that these processes may lead to major benefits in food production and the environment. Furthermore, there is no doubt that some medical advances may have saved millions of lives. However, this level of technology can contain a strong element of risk.

Our ignorance of the long-term effects of releasing GM plants or even animals into the environment means that this step should only be taken after very careful consideration.

Essay extract

It has been claimed that GM technology is no different from breeding techniques which have been practised by man for thousands of years. Source A states that this process is similar to natural selection and remarks: 'such procedures are now labelled "interfering with nature"'. On the other hand Source B considers that, although GM technology could bring considerable benefits in medicine and agriculture, it is quite different to traditional processes of selection. He believes that crossing the species barrier is a dangerous step and that there is insufficient knowledge of the long-term results of such developments.

3. **The essay writer uses a mixture of direct quotes and summaries of arguments.**

    a) *Find an example of each.*

    b) *What phrase does the writer use to mark the point where he moves from dealing with Source A to Source B?*

    c) *List all the phrases used to introduce summaries.*

    It has been claimed that

4. **You are preparing to write an essay titled 'The social effects of tourism in developing countries'.**

    Read the sources and then complete the paragraph comparing their views, as in the example above.

Source C

When countries begin to provide facilities for mass tourism, such as hotels and leisure complexes, there is an immediate demand for labour. Work is created for cleaners, waiters, gardeners and drivers on a scale which may significantly boost the local economy. Such work may provide opportunities to learn valuable new skills. For many, these semi-skilled jobs provide an attractive alternative to subsistence agriculture or fishing, while at the same time the tax revenues from their earnings increase the national income.

Source D

One inevitable feature of tourism's growth is the creation of badly-paid, seasonal jobs in holiday resorts. Much of this work combines insecurity with long hours of work in poor conditions. In Thailand, for example, there are cases of hotel maids working 15-hour days for less than $4. Moreover, the combination of wealthy tourists being served by impoverished workers is likely to increase social tensions in these areas. Another risk is that natural or human disasters such as wars and earthquakes may drive visitors away without warning, leaving tens of thousands unemployed.

Source E

In defence of the tourist industry, it has been claimed that the development of tourism played a major part in helping to modernise parts of Franco's Spain in the 1960s. The presence of easy-going, affluent visitors apparently encouraged locals to learn new skills and open new businesses. Despite this positive interpretation, many examples could be presented where the arrival of rich and idle tourists has been an encouragement for crime, prostitution and other less desirable aspects of the modern economy. Much seems to depend on the economic alternatives offered by the society, and of course the scale of tourist arrivals.

It has been argued that tourism can have a very positive social influence on a developing country. Source C claims that

1.11 Planning Essays

Outline planning was examined in Unit 1.3. Planning gives essays a coherent structure and, most importantly, helps to ensure that they answer the question set. Although all essays need planning, they are written in two different situations: as coursework, and in exams. Clearly, under the time pressure of an exam, planning is more hurried, but can also be more critical. This unit looks first at planning in exams, and then for coursework.

cross-reference

1.3   *From Titles to Outlines*

1. **In the case of essays written in exams, it is best to begin planning by analysing the title and then writing down any ideas that seem relevant. This process is called 'brainstorming', and at first ideas are collected in any order.**

    Read the title below and add more ideas to the list.

    Outline the development of the modern tourist industry.

    • development of passenger jet aircraft in late 1950s

    • package holidays became popular in 1960s

    • increased leisure time in developed countries

    •

    •

    •

cross-reference

1.13   *Organising the Main Body*
2.6   *Discussion*

2. **Having assembled your ideas, it is then necessary to find a suitable framework for the essay. A structure may be suggested by the title of the essay. There are a number of common structures used in essay writing.**

    Which one would be most suitable for the title above?

    a) **Time** – usually from the past to the present or future, as narrative.

    b) **Comparison** – two or more topics are examined and compared, one after the other.

    c) **For and against** – the advantages and disadvantages of two systems are discussed.

3. *Complete the plan using ideas from (1).*

    Outline the development of the modern tourist industry.

    a) Introduction: Current situation: growing demand/current problems, e.g. pollution

    b) Main body:

        i) mass tourism began in 1960s with development of jet aircraft

        ii)

iii)

iv)

c)   Conclusion:

4.   *Decide which of the three structures in (2) would be most suitable for the following titles.*

   a)   Prisons make criminals worse, and should be abolished – discuss.

   b)   In the UK, radio is gaining audience while TV is losing viewers. Consider possible reasons.

   c)   Trace the development of mass production and evaluate its main benefits.

   d)   'Examinations can never be fair.' To what extent is this true?

   e)   The internet will make books redundant in twenty years – discuss.

cross-reference

2.4   *Comparison*

5.   *Study the title below and the ideas collected for the essay. Add to the list if possible. Then choose a suitable framework and complete the plan below.*

   Compare the effects of advertising on TV with advertising in newspapers. What are the main differences? Are there any similarities?

   TV adverts more lively, dynamic

   newspaper adverts can be targeted at a special market, e.g. local

   TV advertising very expensive (to make and show)

   many people video TV and fast forward adverts

   newspaper adverts can be prepared more quickly

   TV adverts can reach a wider audience

   a)   Introduction: role of newspapers and TV in society today

   b)   Main body:

      i)

      ii)

iii)

iv)

c)   Conclusion:

6.   *Choose one of the titles below and note at least six ideas that might be used in the essay. Then select a suitable framework and write a plan.*

a)   In 20 years' time most learning will be on-line: the internet will replace the classroom – discuss.

b)   Describe the education system in your country and suggest how it could be improved.

Ideas
Plan

7.   **In the case of longer essays, written as coursework, planning should be more detailed. It will normally be a two-stage process:**

a)   before reading: using the title to develop an outline structure

b)   after reading: modifying the outline and adding detail

Study the notes below. Use them to write a plan for the title.

Title: Student numbers in higher education are rising in most countries. Is it desirable to keep increasing the numbers of young people who take a degree?

a)   In 1985 12% of young people went to university in the UK. Now the figure is over 30%. Similar growth has been experienced in many countries, developed and developing.

b) Recent research (Jackson *et al.*) shows that employers are looking for personal skills rather than educational qualifications.

c) The average student in Britain now leaves university with debts of £15,000.

d) University education may help students from poorer families to move into a higher social position.

e) Modern economies are based on knowledge. Therefore, every country needs to educate its workforce as highly as possible to compete with other economies.

f) Because increasing numbers of young people are gaining a first degree, their degrees are worth less. It is now necessary to have a second degree to compete in the labour market.

g) As student numbers rise, standards fall. Classrooms become more crowded, and overworked teachers are less able to give students personal attention.

1.12 Organising Paragraphs

Paragraphs are the basic building blocks of texts. Well-organised paragraphs not only help readers understand the argument, they also help writers to structure their ideas effectively.

1.   *Read the following paragraph.*

The way we use banks is currently changing. This is partly because of the introduction of new technology in the last ten years. The personal computer and the internet, for instance, allow customers to view their accounts at home and perform operations such as moving money between accounts. At the same time banks are being reorganised in ways that affect both customers and staff. In the past five years over 3,000 bank branches have closed in Britain. The banks have discovered that staffing call centres is cheaper than running a branch network.

The structure of the paragraph is:

1.	topic sentence	The way we use banks . . .
2.	reason	This is partly because . . .
3.	example	The personal computer . . .
4.	information	At the same time banks . . .
5.	information	In the past five years . . .
6.	reason	The banks have discovered . . .

cross-reference
2.5   Definitions
2.7   Examples
2.12 Restatement and
      Repetition

2.   a)   A paragraph is a collection of sentences which deal with one subject.

b)   All paragraphs contain a **topic** sentence, which is often, but not always, the first.

c)   Other components vary according to the nature of the topic. Introductory paragraphs often contain **definitions**, while descriptive paragraphs include a lot of **information**. Other sentences give **examples** and offer **reasons** and **restatements**.

3.   *Read and analyse the following paragraph.*

In recent years all British universities have adopted the semester system. A semester is a period of time which lasts for half the academic year. Semester 1, for example, starts in September and finishes in January. Previously the academic year had been divided into three terms: autumn, winter and spring. Most courses consist of modules which last for one semester, and exams are held at the end of each. Britain began using semesters to make it easier for international students to move from one country to another.

1.	
2.	
3.	
4.	
5.	
6.	

4.   **The sentences below form a paragraph, but have been mixed up.**

Use the table to rewrite the sentences in the correct order.

a)   The Romans were the first people to build a bridge near the position of today's Tower Bridge.

b)   London has been the English capital for over 1,000 years.

c)   Over 500 years ago the area below the bridge had become a major river port for ships trading with Europe.

d)   Its dominance is due to its strategic site near the lowest crossing point of the River Thames.

e)   For many centuries it has been the centre of the country's economic, cultural and social life.

1.	topic	
2.	restatement	
3.	reason	
4.	example	
5.	information	

cross-reference

2.3   Cohesion

5. **The sentences below form a paragraph, but have been mixed up.**

   Rewrite them in the correct order and analyse the paragraph structure, using the components below.

   Topic 1, Topic 2, Example, Information, Reason

   a) Even simple words like 'dinner' or 'hello' were not recognised.

   b) Consequently, the keepers have been trained to talk French to the baboons.

   c) The zoo realised that the animals were used to hearing commands in French.

   d) An English zoo has been given a gift of nineteen baboons by a zoo in Paris.

   e) But when the English zoo keepers tried speaking to the animals there was no response.

1.	
2.	
3.	
4.	
5.	

cross-reference

1.14   Introductions

6. *You are writing an essay on 'Prisons make criminals worse, and should be abolished'. Using the notes below, complete the introductory paragraph, following the structure provided.*

   Introduction

   Modern prison system developed in nineteenth century

   Prisons intended to isolate, punish and reform

Steep rise in number of prisoners in last 20 years

Critics claim they are 'universities of crime'

Essay aims to consider how effective prisons are

1.	The modern prison system . . .
2.	The system had three basic aims: . . .
3.	However, in the last 20 years . . .
4.	Prisons are commonly criticised . . .
5.	This essay attempts to evaluate . . .

cross-reference

2.6   Discussion

7. *Using the second set of notes, write the next paragraph of the essay.*

    Advantages

    Prisons offer society three apparent benefits

    Provide punishment by deprivation of freedom

    Offenders are segregated so cannot re-offend

    Possibility of reform through training programmes

1.
2.
3.
4.

8. *Using the next set of notes, write the third paragraph.*

    Drawbacks

    Prisons appear to be failing in twenty-first century

    Prison population steadily rising in many countries

    Many prisoners are 'repeat offenders'

    Few prisons able to offer effective reform programmes

    Prison conditions often brutal and degrading

1.	
2.	
3.	
4.	
5.	

cross-reference

1.15   Conclusions

9. *Write a concluding paragraph, summarising the previous points and using your own ideas, to answer the title given.*

1.13 Organising the Main Body

This and the next two units deal with the organisation of the main body, the introduction and the conclusion. In the case of longer assignments it is often better to write the main body before the introduction. With shorter essays, for example in exams, this is impractical, and the introduction has to be written first.

cross-reference

1.11   *Planning Essays*

1. **The structure of the main body depends on the length of the essay and the subject of study.**

   Shorter essays (in exams, for example) tend to have simpler structures:

   Description/ development $A \longrightarrow B \longrightarrow C \longrightarrow D$

   For and against

   $$X \quad Y \qquad or \qquad X \quad Y$$
   $$X1 \quad Y1 \qquad\qquad X1 \longrightarrow Y1$$
   $$X2 \quad Y2 \qquad\qquad X2 \longrightarrow Y2$$

   Comparison/evaluation

   $$J \quad K \quad L$$
   $$J1 \longrightarrow K1 \longrightarrow L1$$
   $$J2 \longrightarrow K2 \longrightarrow L2$$

   Match the examples of plans for main bodies below to the structures above.

   a) Prisons make criminals worse, and should be abolished – discuss.

      i) benefit of prisons – deterrence

      ii) benefit of prisons – removes dangerous people from society

      iii) drawback of prisons – prisoners lose contact with non-criminal society

      iv) drawback of prisons – prisoners become bitter and learn criminal techniques

   b) In the UK, radio is gaining audience while TV is losing viewers. Consider possible reasons.

      i) radio can be listened to in many situations

      ii) radio offers a wide variety of programme types

      iii) TV lacks flexibility, needs full attention

      iv) economic factors: TV more expensive to buy/ programmes more expensive to make

   c) Trace the development of the factory system and describe its social impact.

      i) factories originally sited to make use of water power (in eighteenth century)

ii)   first factories employed unskilled workers; often women and children

iii) in nineteenth century factories built near canals/railways for access to markets

iv)   later some employers offered social benefits, e.g. housing/education

cross-reference

2.1   *Argument*

2.   **Inside the main body, ideas need to be presented in the most logical fashion, linked together to form a coherent argument.**

Select a suitable structure from (1) and reorganise the notes below in the best order.

Lowering the minimum school leaving age to 14 would allow teachers to focus on teaching the students who wanted to be in school – discuss.

if they left at 14, students would be unlikely to find proper jobs

some students more suited to work which doesn't require qualifications

problem students waste everybody's time, including their own

effort should be made in primary schools to prevent pupils falling behind

many older students have lost interest in learning and disrupt classes

in future, almost all jobs will demand academic skills

3.   **Longer essays may include the following sections:**

Literature review – a summary of the main authorities on this topic

Experimental set-up – a technical description of the organisation of an experiment

Methods – how the research was carried out

Findings/results – what was discovered by the research/experiment

Case study – a description of an example of the topic being researched

Discussion – an examination of the issues and the writer's verdict

The sections below constitute the main body of an essay titled 'Studying abroad: an analysis of costs and benefits'. Decide on the heading of each section and the best order (1–5) for them.

a)   Comparisons of the advantages and disadvantages that students mentioned about study abroad and an attempt to decide if most students benefited from the experience.

b)   Aims of the survey and how the researcher conducted it.

c)   An extensive study of two students (from different cultures) studying in Britain who were interviewed by the researcher.

d)   A report of what the survey found, with statistical analysis.

e)   A synopsis of the recent published research in this area.

cross-reference

3.7   *Conjunctions*

4.   **Special phrases can be used to mark the beginning of new paragraphs, or the introduction of new topics.**

To introduce a new paragraph/topic:

The main/chief factor/issue is . . .

Turning to the subject of . . .

Moving on to the question of . . .

Another important area is . . .

. . . . should also be examined

To add information inside a paragraph:

a)   Firstly, . . .   The first point . . .   In the first place . . .

b)   Secondly, . . .   Next, ...   Then, . . .
     In addition . . .   Moreover . . .

c)   Finally, . . .   Lastly, . . .

5.   *Complete the following extract from an essay on 'British weather' with suitable phrases.*

The British are famous all over the world for their obsession with the weather, but in fact the reality is more complex than is often believed. This essay sets out to examine some of the principal influences on the weather of the British Isles.

. . . . is the geographical position of Britain, situated on the extreme western edge of the European continent. This means that a variety of weather types can dominate the country. . . . . the Atlantic Ocean can produce warm wet winds, especially in winter. . . . . the land mass of Europe can create anticyclonic weather, hot in summer and cold in winter. . . . . the polar region to the north can generate cold winds at most seasons of the year.

. . . . variations within Britain, there are significant differences between regions. . . . . the south of England can be much warmer than the north of Scotland, especially in winter. . . . . the west of Britain is usually much wetter than the east. . . . . even in the same district, hilly areas will be cooler and wetter than the lowlands.

. . . . is seasonal change, which in Britain is less distinct than in many countries. . . . . the Atlantic moderates extreme types of weather, and . . . . the weather pattern can change radically from year to year. As a result warm days in winter and chilly summer winds frequently surprise visitors to this country.

1.14 Introductions

An introduction is crucial, not just for what it says about the topic, but for what it tells the reader about the writer's style and approach. Unless you can introduce the subject clearly the reader may not wish to continue.

1. *What is the purpose of the introduction to an essay? Choose from the items below:*

    a) to define some of the terms in the title

    b) to give your opinion of the subject

    c) to show that you have read some research on the subject

    d) to show that the subject is worth writing about

    e) to explain which areas of the subject you will deal with

    f) to get the reader's attention with a provocative idea

    g) to show how you intend to organise your essay

2. *Study the extracts from introductions below, and decide which of the functions in the box they fulfil.*

i)	explain starting point for research
ii)	state aims/goals
iii)	refer to recent research in same area
iv)	give results of research
v)	provide background information
vi)	concede limitations

    a) In many companies, the knowledge of most employees remains untapped for solving problems and generating new ideas.

    b) This paper positions call centres at the core of the mix of technologies public administration can use to innovate e-commerce.

    c) In fact, this is one of our main findings based on an extended sample period up to 1998.

    d) Admittedly, the tenor of my argument is tentative and exploratory.

    e) The purpose of this paper is to investigate changes in the incidence of extreme warm and cold temperatures over the globe since 1870 . . .

f)   To what extent do increases in the food available per person at a national level contribute to reductions in child malnutrition? This question has generated a wide range of responses (Haddad *et al.*, 1997).

2.5   *Definitions*

3.   **There is no such thing as a standard introduction, and much depends on the nature of the research and the length of the essay. However, for a relatively short essay written under exam conditions, the following are worth including, in this order.**

a)   Definitions of any terms in the title that are unclear

b)   Some background information

c)   Reference to other writers who have discussed this topic

d)   Your purpose in writing and the importance of the subject

e)   Any limitations, e.g. geographical or chronological, that you set yourself

f)   A summary of the main points you intend to cover

a)   It may be necessary to clarify some of the words in the title. This may be because they are not in common use or have a specialised meaning.

Discuss the Impact of Privatisation on the British Economy.

Privatisation is the process of transferring certain industries from state control to the private sector, which began in Britain in 1981 with British Telecom . . .

b)   Background information helps to give a context for your essay.

In recent years the privatisation of state owned businesses, especially monopoly utilities such as electricity and telecoms, has become widespread in both developed and developing nations.

c)   It is important to show that you are familiar with current research. This can be demonstrated using phrases such as:

A number of researchers have examined this issue, notably . . .

Various investigations have explored the subject, especially . . .

d)   You must show the importance of the topic. This can be either in the academic world, or as a contemporary issue of wider relevance.

As privatisation is increasingly seen as a remedy for economic ills in many other countries, it is worth examining its impact in Britain, which was a pioneer in this process.

e) As you are only writing an essay, not a book, it is obviously not possible to deal with all aspects of your subject. Therefore you need to explain what limits you are setting on the discussion, and possibly give reasons for this.

Only privatisations completed between 1981–95 will be dealt with, as it is too soon to assess the impact of later developments.

f) For your own benefit, as well as the reader's, it is useful to outline how the essay will be organised.

An assessment will first be made of the performance of the privatised industries themselves, on an individual basis, and then the performance of the economy as a whole will be examined.

cross-reference
2.6   Discussion

4. *Prepare to write an introduction to an essay with the title 'Higher education should be available to everyone – discuss' by answering the questions below.*

a) Which terms in the title might need defining?

b) What background information could you give?

c) How can you show the current relevance of this topic, either in Britain or another country?

d) How are you going to limit your discussion: geographically, historically or both?

e) How will you organise the main body of the essay?

(As this is a short essay, it is not necessary to mention sources in the introduction.)

5. *Write the introduction (about 100 words) in the space below, using your answers from (4) and the notes provided below.*

Definition:	Higher education (HE) = university education
Background:	Increasing demand for HE worldwide puts pressure on national budgets > many states seek to shift costs to students
Relevance:	In most countries degree = key to better jobs and opportunities
Discussion points:	If students have to pay more of cost, discriminates against poorer families
	Is it fair for all taxpayers to support students?
	How to keep HE open to able students from all backgrounds?

6. *Write an introduction to an essay on one of the following titles, or choose a subject from your own discipline.*

    a) Compare the urbanisation process in the First and the Third Worlds.

    b) Assess the importance of public transport in the modern city.

    c) 'Lawyers are inflating the cost of medicine' – discuss.

    d) To what extent is a democratic system necessary for economic development?

1.15 Conclusions

1. **Not every academic essay has a conclusion. In some cases it may be linked to the discussion section, or it may be called 'concluding remarks', or 'summary'. However, in most cases it is helpful for the reader to have a section which (quite briefly) looks back at what has been said and makes some comments about the main part.**

   Read the following extracts from conclusions and match them with the list of functions in the box.

   ---

   i) comparisons with other studies

   ii) summary of main body

   iii) limitations of research

   iv) suggestions for further research

   v) practical implications and proposals

   ---

   a) In this review, attempts have been made to summarise and assess the current research trends of transgenic rice dealing exclusively with agronomically important genes.

   b) As always, this investigation has a number of limitations to be considered in evaluating its findings.

   c) Obviously, business expatriates could benefit from being informed that problem focused coping strategies are more effective than symptom focused ones.

   d) Another line of research worth pursuing further is to study the importance of language for expatriate assignments.

   e) Our review of thirteen studies of strikes in public transport demonstrates that the effect of a strike on public transport ridership varies and may either be temporary or permanent . . .

   f) These results of the Colombia study reported here are consistent with other similar studies conducted in other countries (Baron and Norman, 1992).

   g) To be more precise, there was a positive relation between tolerant and patient problem solving and all four measures of adjustment: general, interaction, work and subjective well-being.

h) To empirically test this conjecture, we need more cross-national replication of this research.

2. *Compare the following conclusions to two essays on 'Public transport in a modern economy'. Complete the table to show the main differences between them.*

a) As has been shown, public transport is likely to play an important role in the future. Despite possible changes in patterns of work and leisure, it seems likely that mass transport systems will remain necessary for the efficient movement of people. What is not clear is how such transport systems should be funded. Various schemes have been discussed, but the most effective model will probably contain some element of public funding. Market forces alone are unlikely to provide a satisfactory solution. This is in broad agreement with the views of most other recent commentators, notably Tilic (1998) and Vardy (2002).

b) In such a brief study it is hard to draw definite conclusions about the future shape of public transport. In addition space has not permitted an examination of the situation in Asia, where significant growth of public transport has taken place. The main areas of debate have been outlined, but much more research is needed before firm conclusions can be drawn. Whether public transport flourishes or deteriorates in future is still unclear, though further studies, especially in the field of public/private partnerships, may eventually suggest an answer.

a	
b	

3. **As illustrated in (1), the following components may be found in conclusions.**

Decide on the most suitable order for them (1–5).

Implications of the findings

Proposals for further research

Limitations of the research

Reference to how these findings compare with other studies

Summary of main findings

4. *Below are notes for the main body of an essay. Read the notes and complete the conclusion, using your own ideas if necessary.*

    Cultural adaptation among overseas students at an Australian university.

    a) **The research programme**

        purpose: to study how students from different cultural backgrounds adapt to academic life in Australia

        size and method: 250 questionnaires returned (30% Chinese, 25% SE Asian, 20% Middle Eastern, 25% other)

    b) **Findings** – culture was only one factor in determining successful adaptation

        Other important factors: age/previous experience of living abroad/language proficiency

    c) **Discussion** – how accurate was research? How could it have been improved? What can be done to help students adapt better?

Summary	The aim of the study was to explore differing degrees of adjustment to life at an Australian university among overseas students from a variety of cultural backgrounds. 250 valid questionnaires were completed, representing about a third of the overseas student population, with significant numbers of Chinese, SE Asian and Middle Eastern students. The results suggest
Implications	
Limitations	
Proposals for further research	

cross-reference

2.4   Comparison

5. **Study the notes for the essay below and write a conclusion in about 100 words.**

A comparison of classroom learning with internet-based teaching.

a) Reasons for increasing use of on-line education:

cheaper if large numbers involved

allows students to study in their own time

students do not have to travel to university

b) Reasons why classroom based education remains popular:

students can be part of group; receive support and advice; learn from colleagues

students have face-to-face contact with a teacher

is seen as traditional and effective

c) Discussion

can a solitary student in front of a computer enjoy the same learning experience as a member of a class?

pressure of numbers in universities makes more on-line education likely

is internet learning really a new method of education? Distance learning has been popular for many years (e.g. Open University)

1.16 Rewriting and Proof-reading

When you have finished the conclusion it may be tempting to hand in your work immediately. However, it is almost certain that it can be improved by being revised. With longer assignments, it may be worth asking a classmate to read your work and make criticisms. Proof-reading is a vital final step, which can prevent confusion or misunderstanding due to simple errors. Computer programs that check spelling will not detect other common types of mistakes.

Rewriting

1. **After finishing the first draft of an essay you should, if you have time, wait for a while and then re-read it, asking the following questions.**

    a) How well does this answer the question in the title?

    b) Have I forgotten any points which would strengthen the development?

    c) Is it clearly structured and well linked together?

cross-reference

2.4   Comparison
4.5   Comparison Essay

2. *Read this short essay written by a Japanese student on the title 'Compare the university system in your country with the British system'. Answer the questions above as you read.*

    It is said that there are large differences in the teaching methods between British universities and Japanese ones. Courses in British universities consist mainly of lectures, discussions, presentations and tutorials and students study specifically their major subject. On the other hand, Japanese universities normally only have lectures in the first two years and students have to study a wide range of subjects in addition to their major. The aim of this essay is to compare and analyse each system.

    In British universities, students need a more active attitude in their study than Japanese students. They need to prepare for presentations and discussions. This is useful for learning because they take much time for study outside the classroom and as they become familiar with their subjects they will become more interested in them.

    In Japan, students' attitude is amazingly passive and they study only just before exams.

    The other difference between British universities and Japanese ones is, as mentioned above, British students concentrate on their major subject and gain specific knowledge about it. Japanese students, however, gain wider knowledge by studying a few other subjects in addition to their major. This system gives students apparently much knowledge but they cannot study their major deeply and their knowledge is wide-ranging but not useful.

In conclusion, British teaching methods give students more chance to know the subject thoroughly compared to Japanese teaching methods, but Japanese methods are suitable for students who are eager to gain a wide range of knowledge and like to study on their own. It is hard to say which is better, it depends on students.

3.   **A careful re-reading of the essay would suggest the following points.**

a)   The essay only partly answers the title. It looks at university life from a student's position, but does not really deal with the 'system' as a whole. The last line of the conclusion discusses a question not asked in the title.

b)   To deal with the subject more fully the writer needs to examine topics such as length of courses, funding of students and admission procedures. If there is not space to discuss these in detail they must be at least mentioned, to show that the writer is aware that they are central to the subject.

c)   The introduction needs to be more general. It goes straight to a comparison of teaching methods. This could be in the main body. Otherwise the essay is well organised and quite logical.

1.14   *Introductions*

4. *Use the notes below to rewrite the introductory paragraph. (NB It is not necessary to include more details than are given below.)*

> university education important in both UK and Japan (over 30% 18-year-olds)
>
> main points for comparison
>
>> a)   admissions
>>
>> b)   length of courses: first and higher degrees
>>
>> c)   teaching methods
>>
>> d)   assessment
>>
>> e)   financial support
>
> essay will examine each point and analyse differences between countries

> *In both Britain and Japan, university education is undertaken by a significant number (more than 30%) of all young people after leaving school.*

Proof-reading

5. Before handing in any piece of written work for marking, it is important to check it carefully for errors which may distort your meaning or make your work difficult to understand.

    The following examples each contain **one** *common type of error. Underline the error and match it to the list of error types in the box.*

i) factual	v) vocabulary	ix) missing word
ii) word ending	vi) spelling	x) unnecessary word
iii) punctuation	vii) singular/ plural	
iv) tense	viii) style	

    a) The natural poorness of Japan has been overcome . . .

    b) In 1980 in the United States there is 140,000 people who . . .

    c) Actually, hardly any of these has succeeded . . .

    d) . . . to choose the most suitable area in which they can success.

    e) Chinese history reflects in real social and cultural changes.

    f) The highest rate of imprisonment was regestred in the USA . . .

    g) Malaria is on the increase in countries such as Africa . . .

    h) I am very interested in German economy . . .

    i) . . . the french system is quite different.

    j) You don't always know which method is best.

6. When proof-reading it is a good idea to exchange texts with another student, since you may become overfamiliar with your own work. However, even in exam conditions, when this is not possible, it is vital to spend a few minutes checking through your work as this may reveal careless errors that can be quickly corrected.

    Underline and correct the errors in the extracts below (one or two in each).

    a) The graph shows changes in the number of prisoners over 5 years (1930–80).

b)   . . . the way the government prepares his citizens to contribute in the development . . .

c)   Secondly, education not only teach people many knowledge . . .

d)   However, weather it is the most important factor is the issue . . .

e)   There has been a sharp decrease between 1930 and 1950.

f)   The quality of a society depends in the education level.

g)   America had the biggest figure for crime . . .

7.   **Proof-reading a longer text is more difficult. The following is an extract from an essay comparing university education in Taiwan and the UK.**

Correct any errors you find.

There are many similarities to the UK and Taiwan, for example course fees, assessment and so on. Firstly, both UK universities and Taiwan universities charge fees from students, but course fees in the UK is as expensive as that in Taiwan. In addition, teaching methods are very similar to both of countries. Students should attend lectures and seminars. Moreover, they have the same system to assess students, which are examed at the end of semester. Nevertheless, there are three main differences: how students can entry a university and how much percentage of students are in higher education. Students in higher education in Taiwan are twice more than in the UK

2. Elements of Writing

Student Introduction

The *Elements of Writing* are the various skills that are needed for most types of academic writing, whether it is a short report, a long essay or a dissertation. Many essays, for instance, begin by defining a term in the title (unit 2.5 *Definitions*), then make some generalisations about the subject (unit 2.8 *Generalisations*) before going on to give examples of the main areas the writer wishes to examine (unit 2.7 *Examples*). Throughout the essay the writer needs to provide references to sources used (unit 2.11 *References and Quotations*) and to employ an appropriate academic style (unit 2.13 *Style*). Many academic subjects also require discussion of statistics (unit 2.9 *Numbers*), and graphs and charts (unit 2.16 *Visual Information*).

In the case of unit 2.4 *Comparison* and unit 2.6 *Discussion*, students should note that the comparison or discussion might apply to the overall pattern of the essay or to just one section. It is common, for instance, for longer essays to have a discussion section before the conclusion.

There is no fixed order for working on the units in *Elements of Writing*. They are organised alphabetically for easy access, and most students will have their own priorities. As in Part 1, the cross-reference boxes provide links to other relevant units.

2.1 Argument

1. *Study the organisation of the following paragraph:*

> Currently, roads are often congested, which is expensive in terms of delays. It is claimed that building more roads, or widening existing ones, would ease the congestion. But not only is the cost of such work high, but the construction process adds to the congestion, while the resulting extra road space may encourage extra traffic. Therefore constructing extra roads is unlikely to solve the problem, and other remedies, such as road pricing or greater use of public transport, should be examined.

a)	**Problem**	*Currently, roads are often congested, which is . . .*
b)	**Solution A**	*It is claimed that building more roads, or widening . . .*
c)	**Argument against solution A**	*But not only is the cost of such work high, but . . .*
d)	**Solutions B and C**	*. . . other remedies, such as road pricing or greater use . . .*

2. *The same ideas could be presented to arrive at a different conclusion:*

> Currently, roads are often congested, which is expensive in terms of delays. It is claimed that building more roads is costly, increases congestion and will encourage extra traffic. This may be partly true, but the alternatives are equally problematic. Road pricing has many practical difficulties, while people are reluctant to use public transport. There is little alternative to a road building programme except increasing road chaos.

Problem	*Currently, roads are often congested, which is . . .*
Solution A	*building more roads . . .*
Arguments against solution A	*It is claimed that building more roads is costly, increases . . .*
Solutions B and C and arguments against	*Road pricing has many practical difficulties, while people are . . .*
Conclusion in favour of solution A	*There is little alternative to a road building programme . . .*

3. *Analyse the following paragraph in a similar way:*

> Obesity is a growing problem in many countries. It can lead to various medical conditions which increase the demand for public health services. There is no clear agreement on the causes of the condition, although some doctors blame a sedentary lifestyle. This does not explain why only certain people suffer from the condition, while others are not affected. Another theory is that a high fat diet, linked to modern processed food, is to blame. Recent research shows that most obesity sufferers do eat this unhealthy diet.

Problem	
Cause A	
Argument against cause A	
Cause B	
Conclusion in favour of B	

4. *Use the following points to build an argument in one paragraph:*

Topic:	University expansion
Problem:	Demand for university places is growing, leading to overcrowding
Solution A:	Increase fees to reduce demand
Argument against A:	Unfair to poorer students
Solution B:	Government pays to expand universities
Argument against B:	Unfair to average taxpayer who would be subsidising the education of a minority who will earn high salaries
Conclusion:	Government subsidises poorer students

5. *Think of a similar debate in your own subject. Complete the
    table and write a paragraph which leads to a conclusion.*

Topic	
Problem	
Solution A	
Argument against A	
Solution B	
Argument against B	
(Solution C)	
Conclusion	

2.2 Cause and Effect

cross-reference

3.20   *Verbs – Passives*

1. **The relationship between two situations can be shown in a variety of ways:**

Heavy rain *causes* flooding.

Heavy rain *leads to* flooding.

Heavy rain *results in* flooding.

Heavy rain *produces* flooding.

Flooding *is caused by* heavy rain. (note use of passive)

Flooding *is produced by* heavy rain.

Flooding *results from* heavy rain.

cross-reference

3.7   *Conjunctions*

2. **It is also possible to use conjunctions which demonstrate cause and effect.**

Cause	Effect
because (of)	so
since	therefore
as	consequently
owing to	which is why
due to	

Because it rained heavily, the flooding was severe.
(because + verb)

The flooding occurred *because of* days of heavy rain.
(because + noun)

As/since it rained heavily, the flooding was severe.
(conjunction + verb)

Owing to/due to the heavy rain the flooding was severe.
(conjunction + noun)

(also: Owing to it raining . . .)

It rained heavily for days, *therefore* the flooding was severe. (used in mid-sentence)

NB It is more common to use conjunctions to illustrate particular situations.

3. *Decide whether the following are particular or general, then complete them with a suitable verb or conjunction.*

   a) Childhood vaccination . . . . reduced infant mortality.

   b) . . . . the cold winter hospital admissions increased.

   c) Printing money . . . . higher inflation.

   d) The summer was extremely dry, ... many trees died.

   e) In 2003, falling sales . . . . the company closing two factories.

Write two more sentences from your own subject area.

   f)

   g)

4. *Use conjunctions to complete the following paragraph.*

   WHY WOMEN LIVE LONGER

   Some British scientists now believe that women live longer than men a) . . . . T cells, a vital part of the immune system that protects the body from diseases. Previously, various theories have attempted to explain longer female life expectancy. Biologists claimed that women lived longer b) . . . . they need to bring up children. Others argued that men take more risks, c) . . . . they die earlier. But a team from Imperial College think that the difference may be d) . . . . women having better immune systems. Having studied a group of men and women they found that the body produces fewer T cells as it gets older, e) . . . . the ageing process. However, they admit that this may not be the only factor, and f) . . . . another research project may be conducted.

5. *Study the flowchart and complete the paragraph which describes it.*

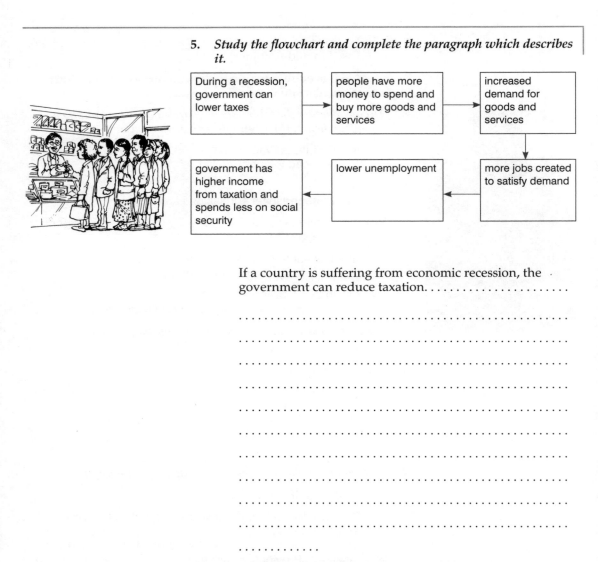

| During a recession, government can lower taxes | → | people have more money to spend and buy more goods and services | → | increased demand for goods and services |

| government has higher income from taxation and spends less on social security | ← | lower unemployment | ← | more jobs created to satisfy demand |

If a country is suffering from economic recession, the government can reduce taxation. . . . .

. . . .

. . . .

. . . .

. . . .

. . . .

. . . .

. . . .

. . . .

. . . .

. . . .

6. *Draw a flowchart similar to the one above, for your own subject, and write a paragraph to describe it.*

2.3 Cohesion

3.7   Conjunctions

1. Cohesion means linking phrases together so that the whole text is clear and readable. It is achieved by several methods, such as the use of conjunctions. Another is the linking of phrases and sentences with words like *he, they* and *that* which refer back to something mentioned before:

> *Jane Austen* wrote six major *novels* in *her* short life. *They* deal

with domestic drama in middle-class families.

Examples of reference words and phrases

Pronouns	he/she/it/they
Possessive pronouns	his/her/hers/their/theirs
Objective pronouns	her/him/them
Demonstrative pronouns	this/that/these/those
Other phrases	the former/the latter/the first/the second

2. *Read the following paragraph and complete the table.*

> *Jenkins* (1987) has researched the life cycle *of new businesses*. *He* found that *they* have an *average life of only 4.7 years*. *This* is due to two main reasons; one *economic* and one *social*. *The former* appears to be a lack of capital, *the latter* a failure to carry out sufficient market research. Jenkins considers that together *these* account for approximately 70% of business failures.

Reference	Reference word/phrase
Jenkins	*he*
new businesses	
average life of only 4.7 years	
one economic	
one social	
the former . . . . ., the latter	

3. *Read the paragraph and complete the table below to show what the reference words (in italics) refer to.*

> There is little prospect of improvement in the standard of living of the villagers from *their* present low level without the support of electricity. Presently, the households can enjoy only a limited number of hours of illumination based on kerosene or diesel. *These* are not cheap and so are not affordable by a large majority of the rural masses. *This* restricts the range as well as the intensity of *their* activities severely. But even if supply of power from *these sources* is available more abundantly, there is the problem of adverse environmental effects of *such use*.

Reference	Reference word
	their
	these
	this
	their
	these sources
	such use

4. *In the following paragraph, insert suitable reference words from the box below in the gaps.*

Disposable razor blades were invented by Gillette at the beginning of the twentieth century. a) . . . . were a simple idea but at first b) . . . . . . found it very hard to sell c) . . . . d) . . . . . . was because nobody had marketed a throw-away product before. However, e) . . . . . . use of advertising to stimulate demand gradually increased sales and before long f) . . . . became a millionaire.

he x 2/his/them/this/they

5. *Complete these paragraphs with suitable reference words from the table in (1).*

A) The Victoria and Albert Museum is in South Kensington in London. a) . . . . is named after Queen Victoria and b) . . . . . . husband, Prince Albert. c) . . . . was made Queen in 1837, and married d) . . . . three years later. e) . . . . . . had a happy marriage which produced nine children. f) . . . . life together was quite simple, although g) . . . . was the queen of the world's most powerful nation. Albert had a serious character, and perhaps h) . . . . major achievement was to organise the Great Exhibition of 1851, the profits from which helped to build the Museum.

B) One group of commentators have little faith in the ability of food availability to improve child nutrition. a) . . . . arguments are supported by the fact that over two-thirds of malnourished children live in countries with food supplies adequate for b) . . . . populations' needs. c) . . . . point to problems of poverty and to non-food factors, such as children's health and the quality of d) . . . . care. e) . . . . belief is that both, but especially f) . . . . (which is increasing in many countries), play a more significant part in malnutrition than is often admitted.

2.4 Comparison

1. **The two basic comparative forms are:**

   The Pacific Ocean is *larger* than the Atlantic.

   His work is *more interesting* than hers.

   a) *-er* is added to one-syllable adjectives (*slow/slower*) and two-syllable adjectives ending in *-y* (*easy/easier*).

   b) *more* . . . . is used with words of two or more syllables.

   careful/more careful   quickly/more quickly

   However, there are some two-syllable words that can use either form:

   simple/simpler/more simple

2. **Comparisons can be made more exact by using *slightly, much, considerably, far* or *significantly* before the comparative:**

   Dickens' novels are *considerably longer* than Austen's.

   The new Mercedes is *slightly more economical* than the old model.

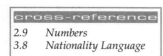

cross-reference	
2.9	*Numbers*
3.8	*Nationality Language*

3. *Study the table and complete the comparisons below.*

   Cost of sending a letter to a domestic destination (Eurocents)

Germany	110
France	85
Japan	62
Britain	60
United States	48
Spain	45

   a) Letters in Japan are . . . . in Britain.

   b) Spanish letters are . . . . German letters.

   c) British letters are . . . . French ones.

   d) Letters in Germany are . . . . in America.

4. **The form *as* . . . . *as* can be used to stress similarity:**

   British letters are nearly *as expensive as* Japanese letters.

   It can also be used for quantitative comparison:

   German letters are *twice as expensive as* American letters.

   (Also: *half as/three times as*/etc.)

5.   **Note the variety of forms possible:**

German letters are more expensive than French (ones/ letters).   (least formal)

Letters in Germany are more expensive than (those) in France.

The cost of sending a letter is higher in Germany than in France.   (most formal)

(*High/low* are used for comparing abstract concepts such as rates.)

Ones can replace the noun when used with an adjective:

German letters are more expensive than Japanese *ones*.

But not in combination with a noun:

Family cars are cheaper than sports cars. (not sports *ones*)

6.   *More/less, the most/the least* **(followed by adjective),** *the most/ the fewest* **(related to number)**

Divorce is *less common* in Greece than in Britain.

The School of Education offers *the most modules*. (more than others)

The most crowded country in Europe is Holland.

NB Superlatives (*most crowded/least visited*) must be defined, e.g. *in Europe/in 1996.*

7.   *Complete the following description of the table above* **(one** *word per gap):*

According to the table, Spain is the a) . . . . expensive country for sending a domestic letter. The USA is b) . . . . more expensive, while the cost in Britain is c) . . . . the same d) . . . . in Japan. France and Germany are the e) . . . . expensive countries, France being 20% cheaper f) . . . . Germany. Overall, posting a letter costs g) . . . . as much in Spain h) . . . . in Germany.

cross-reference

4.5   *Comparison Essay*

8. *Study the table and complete the text below* (one *word per gap*).

American spending on leisure activities, 1997, $billion

Video, audio and computers	80
Books and newspapers	51
Casino gambling	24
Lotteries	18
Recorded music	15
Theme parks	9
Video games	8.5
Spectator sports	6
Cinema tickets	5.5
Racecourse betting	2.5

The table shows that Americans spend the
a) . . . . money ($80 bn) on video, audio and
computer equipment. They spend 40% b) . . . .
on books and newspapers, while casinos, in third place,
are c) . . . . popular d) . . . . lotteries or
recorded music. Americans spend e) . . . . more
on theme parks than f) . . . . video games, and
the cinema, in ninth place, is nearly g) . . . .
popular as spectator sports. The h) . . . . amount
of money is spent on racecourse betting.

9. *Study the table below and complete the paragraph comparing
    life expectancy in European countries* (one *word per gap*).

Country	Adult alcohol intake per year (litres)	Cigarettes smoked per day per adult	Life expectancy in years – male	Life expectancy in years – female
Austria	11.9	4.6	74.2	80.5
Belgium	11.7	4.3	73.8	80.5
Britain	9.4	4.2	74.3	79.5
Denmark	12.1	4.9	73.1	78.2
Finland	8.4	2.2	73.3	80.3
France	14.1	4.0	74.2	82.1
Germany	11.8	5.0	73.7	80.0
Greece	10.4	8.3	75.1	81.4
Italy	9.4	4.2	74.9	81.3
Norway	4.8	1.7	75.4	81.0
Portugal	13.6	4.6	71.4	78.7
Sweden	6.4	2.4	76.7	81.8
Switzerland	11.8	5.6	76.1	82.2
EU average	11.1	4.5	74.1	80.5

The table a) . . . . that Swedish men have the b) . . . . life expectancy in Europe, while women live the c) . . . . in Switzerland. d) . . . . average women in Europe live 6 years longer e) . . . . men. Men in Portugal have f) . . . . lowest life expectancy (71.4 years), while the lowest for women is Denmark (78.2 years), which is g) . . . . less than in Portugal (78.7 years).

10. *Complete the following paragraph comparing cigarette smoking in Europe.*

The table shows considerable variations in cigarette smoking in Europe. The highest rate is . . . .

. . . .

. . . .

. . . .

. . . .

. . . .

. . . .

. . . .

. . . . . .

11. *Write another paragraph comparing alcohol intake in Europe.*

2.5 Definitions

cross-reference

1.14 Introductions

1. **In academic writing, definitions are normally needed in two situations:**

   In introductions, to clarify a word or phrase in the title.

   More generally, to explain a word or phrase which may be either very technical (and so not in normal dictionaries), very recent, or with no widely agreed meaning.

Word	Category	Detail	Use
A *lecture*	is a formal talk	given to a large group,	often used for teaching.
An *assignment*	is a task	often given to students	for teaching or assessment.

2. *Insert suitable category words in the following definitions.*

   a) A *barometer* is a scientific . . . . designed to measure atmospheric pressure.

   b) *Kidneys* are . . . . that separate waste fluid from the blood.

   c) A *multi-national company* is a business . . . . that operates in many countries.

   d) *Reinforced concrete* is a building . . . . consisting of cement, sand and steel rods.

   e) *Bullying* is a pattern of anti-social . . . . found in many schools.

   f) *Recycling* is a . . . . in which materials are used again.

   g) A *recession* is a . . . . of reduced economic activity.

   h) *Post codes* are a . . . . for making mail delivery more efficient.

3. **More complete definitions may be written by adding examples or extra information:**

   A mortgage is a type of loan (which is) used for buying property, in which the lender has the security of the property.

   Complete and extend the following definitions.

   a) Distillation is a . . . . used to . . . .

   b) A psychiatrist is a . . . . who specialises in . . . .

c)   An MSc is a . . . . awarded on completion of
. . . .

d)   A trades union is a(n) . . . . which exists to
protect . . . .

e)   Malaria is a . . . . caused by . . . .
. . . .

f)   Wheat is a . . . . used for . . . .
. . . .

4.   *Study the following examples and underline the term being
defined.*

a)   . . . the definition for a failed project . . . ranges from
abandoned projects to projects that do not meet
their full potential or simply have schedule overrun
problems.

b)   Development is a socioeconomic–technological
process having the main objective of raising the
standards of living of the people.

c)   Electronic commerce is characterised by an absence
of physical proximity between the buyer and seller in
conducting the search, assessment and transaction
stages of a transaction . . .

d)   Bowlby (1982) suggested that attachment is an
organised system whose goal is to make individuals
feel safe and secure.

e)   . . . the non-linear effect called 'self-brightening' in
which large-amplitude waves decay more slowly than
small-amplitude ones.

The examples above illustrate the variety of methods
employed in definitions:

(a) gives various examples which fall into the grouping the
author wishes to examine.

(b), (d) and (e) use category words: *process, system, effect*.

(c) defines the term in a negative way (*an absence*).

(d) quotes a definition from another writer.

3.2   *Academic Vocabulary*

5.   **When writing introductions, it is often helpful to define a
term in the title, even when it may be in common use, to
demonstrate that you have thought about it and that you have
a clear idea what it means in your essay.**

Title: Higher education should be free and open to all
– discuss.

Higher education in Britain means university-level study for first or higher degrees, normally at the age of 18 or above.

Study the following titles, decide which term needs defining in each, and write a definition for **two** *of them.*

a)   Compare the murder rate for countries with capital punishment with those without it.

b)   The department store is a nineteenth-century creation which has no future in the twenty-first century – discuss.

c)   The incidence of post-natal depression appears to be rising. What are the most effective methods of treating the condition?

6.   *Select several terms from your own subject area and write extensive definitions for them.*

2.6 Discussion

4.6   *Discussion Essay*

1. **Many essay titles require the writer to examine both sides of a case, and to conclude by coming down in favour of one side. These may be called 'discussion', 'for and against' or 'argument' essays. For example:**

   a) School uniforms – a step forward or a step back? – discuss.

   b) Discuss the advantages and disadvantages of state control of industry.

   In addition, longer essays often require students to assess the information and ideas they have collected in a discussion section before the conclusion.

   Discussion vocabulary

+	–
benefit	drawback
advantage	disadvantage
a positive aspect	a negative feature
pro (informal)	con (informal)
plus (informal)	minus (informal)
one minor benefit of school uniforms is . . .	a serious drawback to state control is . . .

cross-reference

1.13   *Organising the Main Body*

2. **There are two basic outlines for a discussion essay:**

   i)   School uniforms?

   a) advantages: reduce social inequality/encourage group identity/avoid choice

   b) disadvantages: loss of individuality/expense/ unfashionable

   c) discussion: overall, benefits more valuable in most cases

   ii) School uniforms?

   a) social: emphasises group values – diminishes individual choice

   b) practical: expensive for poor families but easier to get dressed

   c) discussion: overall, benefits more valuable in most cases

3. *Choose one of the titles below and write down as many pros and cons in the box as possible. Then prepare a plan using one of the outlines above.*

a)   Instead of going out to work, mothers should stay at home and look after their children until they are at least 5 – discuss.

b)   Fast food, which is spreading round the world and destroying national cultures, should be resisted. To what extent do you agree?

+	–

Title:

a)

b)

c)

d)

cross-reference

2.1   *Argument*

4.   **Presenting your case.**

It is better to use impersonal phrases rather than 'I think':

It is widely believed that young children need to be with their mothers . . .

Most people consider that fast food is very convenient . . .

It is generally agreed that school uniforms develop a group identity . . .

It is probable/possible that fast food will become more acceptable . . .

This evidence suggests that most children benefit from nurseries . . .

However, if you want to present a minority point of view, you can use the following:

It can be argued that children benefit from a diet of hamburgers.

It has been suggested that school uniforms make children more rebellious.

Some people believe that nursery education damages children.

5. **It is important to show that you are aware of** *counter-arguments*.

   These are the points made by people who oppose your position. Without these your argument will appear one-sided. In a discussion you can present these first, before stating your own views.

   Study the example and write similar sentences about working mothers and fast food using ideas from (3).

Counter-argument	Your position
Although it has been suggested that school uniforms make children more rebellious,	*it is generally agreed that uniforms develop a group identity.*

cross-reference

1.10   *Combining Sources*
2.11   *References and Quotations*

6. **Before giving your own opinion, it is necessary to show that you have read the relevant sources and have studied the evidence. Opinions without evidence have little value.**

   The following paragraph discusses the environmental effects of deforestation.

   Lomborg (2001) claims that the danger of extinction of species has been exaggerated. He says that the number of species had been expected to decline dramatically within the next half century, but maintains that this is unlikely: 'Species . . . seem more resilient than expected.' He points out that in the eastern USA, although 98% of the original forests have been cleared, only one forest bird became extinct in the process. Against this, Brooks (2001) feels that Lomborg is ignoring the true rate of forest loss and the related extinction of species: 'The ongoing wave of extinctions, due primarily to deforestation in the moist tropics, has been widely documented.' It seems that Lomborg, as a statistician, is too dependent on optimistic data, and is ignoring the widespread concerns of wildlife experts.

   The paragraph has the following structure:

Lomborg – summary + quotation
Brooks – summary + quotation
Writer's comment on Lomborg + opinion

7. *Complete the following paragraph, which discusses air pollution, to give an opinion.*

    According to Lomborg (2001), air quality is improving in rich countries. He gives the example of London, where he claims that the air is cleaner now than it has been since 1585, thanks to decreases in smoke and sulphur dioxide. Brooks (2001), however, argues that Lomborg is 'ignoring the more recent global rise in toxic contaminants, now found at high concentrations . . . even in the remote reaches of the Arctic.' It appears that . . . .
    . . . .
    . . . .
    . . . .
    . . . .
    . . . .
    . . . .

8. *List in the box as many ideas as possible for and against the following subject:*

    Industrial development is destroying the quality of our lives – discuss.

+	–

9. *Prepare a plan for this title, using one of the outlines in (2) above.*

    a)

    b)

    c)

    d)

10. *Write an essay on this title, making use of phrases from (4) above.*

2.7 Examples

1. **When writing essays it is often better to support statements by giving examples. Compare the following:**

   a) Many plants and animals are threatened by global warming.

   b) Many plants and animals are threatened by global warming. In southern Britain, *for example*, the beech tree may become extinct within 30 years.

   The second sentence provides concrete details of a plant species, an area and a time scale to support the main statement.

cross-reference

3.7   *Conjunctions*

2. **Phrases for introducing examples include:**

   Many departments, *for instance/for example* engineering, now offer foundation courses.

   (note use of commas)

   A few courses, *such as/e.g.* MBA, require work experience.

   Many universities, *particularly/especially* UK ones, ask overseas students for IELTS scores.

   (note the focus)

   Some subjects are heavily oversubscribed. *A case in point* is medicine.

   (for single examples)

   Use suitable example phrases to complete the following sentences.

   a) As the climate warms, wetland species . . . . frogs may find their habitat reduced.

   b) Some animals can migrate to cooler areas. . . . . are birds, which can move easily.

   c) Many slow-growing plants, trees . . . . , will find it difficult to move to wetter areas.

   d) Certain reptiles, ... snakes, may benefit from drier and warmer summers.

   e) Rising sea levels may bring some advantages . . . . expanding wetland areas.

3. *Find a suitable example for each sentence.*

   Example: Various sectors in the economy are experiencing labour shortages.

   Various sectors in the economy, *for instance engineering*, are experiencing labour shortages.

a) A number of sports have become very profitable due to the sale of television rights.

b) Certain twentieth-century inventions affected the lives of most people.

c) In recent years many women have made significant contributions to the political world.

d) Three-year guarantees are now being offered by most car makers.

e) Certain diseases are proving much harder to combat than was expected 20 years ago.

f) Many musical instruments use strings to make music.

g) Several mammals are currently in danger of extinction.

4. *Read the text below and then insert suitable examples where needed.*

Students who go to study abroad often experience a type of culture shock when they arrive in the new country. Customs which they took for granted in their own society may not be followed in the host country. Even everyday patterns of life may be different. When these are added to the inevitable differences which occur in every country students may at first feel confused. They may experience rapid changes of mood, or even want to return home. However, most soon make new friends and, in a relatively short period, are able to adjust to their new environment. They may even find that they prefer some aspects of their new surroundings, and forget that they are not at home for a while!

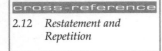

2.12   *Restatement and*
        Repetition

5. **Another small group of phrases is used when there is only one 'example'. This is a kind of restatement:**

> The world's biggest software company, *i.e.* Microsoft, is buying a share of the cable business.

in other words	namely	that is (to say)	i.e.	viz (in very formal English only)

Add a suitable phrase to the following sentences, from the box below, to make them clearer.

a) His mother's sister was a small but very remarkable woman.

b) When the liquid reached boiling point the reaction began.

c) It appears that Candlemas day was celebrated with large bonfires.

d) The company's overheads doubled last year.

> namely 140 degrees
>
> i.e. his aunt
>
> in other words, the fixed costs
>
> that is, February 2nd

2.8 Generalisations

1. **In written work generalisations are very useful because they can be used to present complex ideas or data in a simple form which is easy to understand and remember:**

   > Large companies can offer better career opportunities.
   >
   > Language is an important means of communication.

   Compare the statements on the data in the table below.

   a) 56.2% of British smokers are women.

   b) The majority of British smokers are women.

UK smokers by gender

Men	Women
43.8%	56.2%

   The first sentence is more accurate, but the second, which contains a generalisation, is easier to understand. However, using generalisations does involve a loss of precision, so the writer must judge when they can be used safely, and when it is better to give the full data.

┌─────────────────────┐
cross-reference
3.5   *Caution*
└─────────────────────┘

2. **There are two ways of making a generalisation:**

   a) Using the plural: Computers are useful machines.

   b) Using the singular + definite article: The computer is a useful machine. (less common/more formal)

   It is better to avoid absolute phrases such as *cats are cleverer than dogs*. Instead use more cautious phrases such as *cats tend to be cleverer than dogs* or *most cats are more intelligent than dogs*.

   Write generalisations on the following topics.

   a) child/noise   Example: *Children are often noisy.*

   b) flowers/presents   . . . .
   . . . .

   c) city/pollution   . . . .
   . . . .

   d) fresh fruit/health   . . . .
   . . . .

   e) television/important . . . .
   . . . .

3. *Read the following text and underline the generalisations.*

   > Li Pang is a Chinese student studying architecture in Manchester. He enjoys the style of teaching as well

as the cosmopolitan lifestyle the city provides. Many international students attend British universities. Most welcome the chance to meet classmates from all over the world, and all are pleased to have the chance to improve their English. When he goes home to Shanghai, Li Pang will have a network of international contacts to support his future career.

4.   **Overgeneralising**

cross-reference

2.4   *Comparisons*
2.9   *Numbers*

This means making statements which are too simple or inaccurate. For example, using income figures from the table below, a writer might claim:

People were much richer in 1999 than 20 years earlier.

This ignores inflation over the period. It is more accurate to say:

Average incomes in 1999 were nearly four times higher than in 1979.

Changes in key economic indicators in the UK, 1979–1999

Britain	1979	1989	1999
Inflation rate	13.4%	7.8%	3.4%
Interest rate	12%	13.7%	5.5%
Unemployment	4.1%	6.1%	4.6%
Average income	£5,000	£11,700	£19,000
Average house price	£19,800	£61,500	£68,300

Each of the following contain overgeneralisation. Rewrite them more accurately.

a)   Between 1979 and 1999, the worst period for unemployment was 1989.

b)   Inflation fell steadily for 20 years after 1979.

c)   There was a dramatic rise in house prices in these two decades.

d)   Interest rates peaked in 1989.

5. *Study the table below and complete the generalisations.*

Regional population in 2000 and forecasts for 2100, with % over 60 years old

Region	2000	% over 60	2100	% over 60
N. America	314	16	454	40
W. Europe	456	20	392	45
S. Asia	1,367	7	1,958	35
S. America	515	8	934	33
N. Africa	173	6	333	32

a) By 2100, nearly half the population of W. Europe may
    . . . .

b) The population of N. Africa may . . . .
    . . . .

c) S. Asia and S. America both have . . . .
    . . . .

d) W. Europe is likely to experience a . . . .
    . . . .

e) By 2100, all these regions may . . . .
    . . . .

6. *Read the text on 'Dreams' and write five generalisations using*
    the data.

A recent survey on dreams, completed by over 10,000
people, found that 68% of all dreams came into the
'anxiety' category. Being chased was the most common
dream, recorded by 72%. Dreams about falling (which
signify insecurity) are also very common, being recorded
by 70%.

55% have dreamed about relatives and friends who have
died. Many people believe that dreams can foretell the
future, but only 42% have experienced this type. 28% of
those surveyed have dreams about food, which seem to
occur during periods of weight watching, but 23% have
been pleased by dreams of finding money.

Example: Anxiety seems to be the cause of most dreams.

a) . . . .

b) . . . .

c) . . . .

d) . . . .

e) . . . .

2.9 Numbers

cross-reference

2.16 *Visual Information*

1. **Discussing statistical data is a necessary part of much academic writing:**

> Approximately 1,800 children between the ages of 5 and 12 years were randomly selected . . .

> Already 3% of the US working population (1.55 million) are employed in 70,000 centres . . .

> The earth's atmosphere appears to be gaining 3.3 billion metric tons of carbon annually . . .

> . . . but five winters in the twentieth century were more than 2.4°C colder than average.

Figures and **numbers** are both used to talk about statistical data in a general sense.

> The *figures* in the report need to be read critically.

Digits are individual numbers. Both **fractions** (¹/₂) and **decimals** (0.975) may be used.

> 4,539 – a four-*digit* number

> £225,000 – a six-*figure* salary (a number)

> *Figure (Fig.)* 3 – Infant mortality rates in twelfth century France   (a diagram)

> no final 's' on hundred/thousand/million:

> Six *million* people live in the region.

> but: *Thousands* died in the last outbreak of cholera.

2. **Percentages are commonly used for expressing rates of change:**

Overseas students in the university 2000–2003

2000	2001	2002	2003
200	300	600	1,000

Complete the following sentences about the table above with percentages.

a) Between 2000 and 2001, the number of overseas students increased by . . . . %

b) The number increased by . . . . % the following year.

c) Between 2000 and 2003 there was a . . . . % increase.

3. **Too many statistics can make texts harder to read. In some cases, where the actual number is unimportant, words or phrases may replace numbers to simplify the text:**

> *Forty-three* villages were cut off by the heavy snowstorm.

Dozens of villages were cut off by the heavy snowstorm.

The following words or phrases can be used to describe quantity.

Few students attended her lecture. (less than expected)

Several bodies have been discovered under the temple floor. (3–4)

Various attempts were made to explain the symbols. (3–6)

Dozens of politicians attended the opening ceremony. (30–60)

Scores of books are published every week. (50–100)

Rewrite the following sentences using one of the words or phrases above.

a) Only four people responded to the questionnaire.

b) They received nearly 100 applications for the post.

c) She made five or six proposals to improve the team's performance.

d) He found over fifty factual errors in the article.

e) They made three or four drafts before writing the final report.

4. *Study the following expressions, which are also used to simplify statistics.*

one in three	a third/a quarter
twice (2×)/three times as many	the majority/minority
a tenfold increase	50%, a percentage
to double/halve	on average/the average number
the most/least	a small/large proportion

Rewrite each sentence in a simpler way, using one of the expressions above.

a) Of the 415 people interviewed, 308 said that they supported the president.

b) Last year the number of students on the course was twenty-four, the year before it was twenty and this year it is twenty-two.

c) In 1965 a litre of petrol cost 10p, while the price is now 80p.

d) Out of eighteen students in the group, twelve were women.

e) The new type of train reduced the journey time to Madrid from 7 hours to 3 hours 20 minutes.

f) Fifteen of the students studied law, eight finance and three engineering.

g) The numbers applying to this department have risen from 350 last year to 525 this year.

5. *Rewrite the following sentences to present the data in a simpler way.*

a) The population of the European part of the former Soviet Union is declining rapidly. It is forecast to fall by 18 m to 220 m in 2025, and to drop to 140 m by 2100.

Example:

The population of the European part of the former Soviet Union is forecast to fall by nearly 10% by 2025, and by nearly 40% by the end of the century.

b) The numbers of visitors to the temples show a remarkable pattern. In 1998 just 40,000 made the journey, 83,000 in 1999 and 171,000 in 2000.

c) More than 80% of British students complete their first
    degree course; in Italy the figure is 35%.

d) Tap water costs 0.07p per litre while bottled water, on
    average, costs 50p per litre.

e) Only 8% of the women surveyed believed that they had
    the same rights as men. A considerable 37% complained
    that they had far fewer rights.

f) Life expectancy for men in the UK rose from 49 to 74
    during the twentieth century.

g) The same operation cost £1,850 at a hospital in Blackburn,
    £2,400 in Birmingham and £2,535 in London.

h) In 1086 about 15% of England was forested, compared
    with only 4.8% in 1870.

2.10 Opening Paragraphs

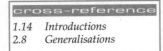

1.14   Introductions
2.8   Generalisations

1. It is often difficult to begin writing an essay, but, especially in exams, hesitation can waste valuable time. The first few sentences need to be general but not vague, as they set the tone for the rest of the essay. The subject can be introduced by giving some background information:

    > In recent years the internet has become an important tool of academic research.

    > There is increasing interest in the use of wind power to produce electricity.

    These statements tend to consist of:

Time phrase	Topic	Development
In recent years	the internet	has become an important tool of academic research.
There is an increasing interest in	the use of wind power	to produce electricity.

These generalisations can be followed by further information or examples:

> In recent years the internet has become an important tool of academic research. Students and teachers find it convenient, accessible and up to date.

> There is increasing interest in the use of wind power to produce electricity. In north Wales, for example, one wind farm generates enough power to light 100,000 homes. Wind power is a renewable resource which does not produce carbon dioxide.

2. *Write two or three introductory sentences on* **one** *of the following topics.*

    a) Global warming

    b) The spread of Aids

    c) The future of the United Nations

    d) Tourism

3. **It is important to begin an essay with remarks that are general but also accurate and clear.**

   Decide which of the following are suitable (essay titles in brackets):

   a) (Do newspapers have a future?)

   Newspapers are facing increased competition from other media such as television and the internet. Young people often prefer to get information from electronic sources, which can be updated more frequently.

   b) (Is public concern about crime justified?)

   Crime is increasing everywhere, and this worries many people. Nobody can agree on a solution to the problem.

   c) (GM foods can feed the world – discuss.)

   In the past twenty years genetically modified (GM) crops have become a source of major controversy. Both farmers and consumers are divided on questions of health and environmental safety.

   d) (Is quality being sacrificed for quantity in higher education?)

   It can be seen that higher education (HE) is changing throughout the world, with more students wanting to enter universities. There are many possible reasons for these changes, but the results are the same.

4. **Having provided some background, the writer should next mention the main areas which will be covered in the essay.**

   Do newspapers have a future?

   Newspapers are facing increased competition from other media such as television and the internet. Young people often prefer to get information from electronic sources, which can be updated more frequently. As a result newspaper sales are declining in many countries. Yet printed news media have certain advantages, such as cheapness and flexibility. In order to survive they are likely to concentrate more on entertainment and comment. In this essay the strengths and weaknesses of newspapers will be examined first, and these will then be compared with their rivals.

5. *Study the following essay titles. Choose two and write an opening paragraph for each in no more than five minutes per paragraph.*

    a) Television can damage the development of children – discuss.

    b) Mature students get better academic results than young students – discuss.

    c) The greatest social change in the twentieth century was the movement of women out of the home and into the workforce. How true is this statement?

2.11 References and Quotations

cross-reference

1.2   *Avoiding Plagiarism*

1. **A reference is an acknowledgement that you are making use of another writer's ideas or data in your writing:**

   > As Donner (1997) pointed out, low inflation does not always lead to low interest rates.

   There are three main reasons for giving references:

   a) To avoid the charge of **plagiarism**, which is using another person's ideas or research without acknowledgement.

   b) The reference can give more authority to your writing, as it shows you are familiar with other research on the topic.

   c) The reader can find the original source by using the reference section which will list the full publishing details of Donner's book:

   > Donner, F. (1997) *Macroeconomics.* Borchester: Borchester University Press

2. *Decide which of the following need references.*

   a) A mention of facts or figures from another writer

   b) An idea of your own

   c) Some data you have found from your own research

   d) A theory suggested by another researcher

   e) A quotation from a work by any author

   f) Something which is agreed to be common knowledge

cross-reference

1.7   *Note-making*

3. **In order to give references accurately it is important to use the following procedure:**

   a) When reading and note-making, keep a careful record of the details of your sources. For a long piece of writing such as a dissertation a card index is useful.

   b) Find out which system of referencing is used in your subject area. You can do this by studying current textbooks and journals and checking departmental guidelines.

   c) Follow one of the methods illustrated below to give the reference.

4. a) **Summary of a writer's ideas**

   > Orwell (1940) pointed out that although Charles Dickens described eating large meals in many of his books, he never wrote about farming. He explains this contradiction in terms of Dickens' upbringing in London, remote from the countryside.

b) **Quotation of a writer's words.**

Orwell clearly highlighted this inconsistency in Dickens: 'It is not merely a coincidence that Dickens never writes about agriculture and writes endlessly about food. He was a Cockney, and London is the centre of the earth in rather the same sense that the belly is the centre of the body.' (Orwell, 1940: pp. 53–4)

c) **Mixture of summary and quotation.**

As Orwell (1940) noted, Dickens frequently described food but was uninterested in food production. He considered that this was because of the writer's background: 'He was a Cockney, and London is the centre of the earth.' (pp. 53–4)

5. *Read the following extract from the same essay* ('Charles Dickens' in *Inside the Whale*, Orwell, G., 1940: pp. 54–5)

What he does not noticeably write about, however, is *work*. In Dickens' novels anything in the nature of work happens off-stage. The only one of his heroes who has a plausible profession is David Copperfield, who is first a shorthand writer and then a novelist, like Dickens himself. With most of the others, the way they earn their living is very much in the background.

a) *Write a summary of the author's ideas, including a suitable reference.*

b) *Introduce a quotation of the key part of the extract, again referring to the source.*

c) *Combine (a) and (b), again acknowledging the source.*

cross-reference

3.22 *Verbs of Reference*

6. **Referring verbs use both the present and the past tenses. It is probably best to use the present tense for recent sources or when you feel that the idea or data is still valid:**

Rathbone (1997) demonstrates the limitations of video-conferencing.

The past tense suggests that the source is older and the ideas perhaps out of date:

Steinbeck (1965) explored a link between cancer and diet.

7. **There are three main systems of reference in use in academic writing:**

a) The system illustrated above (the Harvard) is the most common. Note the following:

Hunter (1989) states . . . (date of publication in brackets when referring verb is used)

Women pose less security risk (Burke and Pollock, 1993)
(authors and date in brackets after summary)

Note that with quotations page numbers should also be given after the date. Details of the organisation of the reference section are given in (8) below.

b)   Numbers in brackets are inserted in the text for each source, and at the end of the chapter or article the references are listed in number order:

A survey of Fortune 500 companies found that over 70% have problems recruiting skilled staff (1). Some analysts argue that this could be as high as 90% (2).

1. Cuervo D. 1990, 'Whither Recruitment?' *HR Journal* **13,** pp. 23–39.

2. Segall, N. 1996, *Cross-cultural studies*, Harper & Row, New York pp. 173–4.

c)   A third system uses footnotes:

More than 80% of families own or are buying their own homes.[2]

In this system the references are listed at the bottom of the page:

[2]*Economist*, 13 January 1996, pp. 27–8.

NB A full reference section is required at the end of the article or book.

8.   **Organising the bibliography/references**

Here is the reference section of an essay written by a business student.

Study the pattern of organisation and answer the following questions.

a)   How are the entries ordered?

b)   What is the difference between the information provided for

  i)   a book by one author

  ii)   a chapter in an edited book

  iii)   a source on the internet

  iv)   an article in a journal

c)   When are *italics* used?

d)   How are capital letters used in titles?

e)   How is a source with no given author listed?

REFERENCES

Brzeski, W. (1999) *The Polish Housing Market* www.onet.pl (Access date 15 Feb. 2000).

Hill, S. (1989) *Managerial Economics, The Analysis of Business Decisions.* London: Macmillan Education Ltd. pp. 100–35.

Koutsoyiannis, A.P. (1963) 'Demand function for tobacco' in Wagner, L. (ed) *Readings in Applied Microeconomics.* Oxford: Oxford University Press.

Mintel Database (2000), *Retail Coffee Market in the UK* (31 Jan. 2000) Available via Warwick University Library (Access date 20 Feb. 2000).

Pass, C. and Lowes, B. (1997) *Business and Microeconomics.* London: Routledge pp. 16–40.

Peck, S. (2000) *Managerial Economics Course Notes.* Warwick Business School.

Russell, T. (1995) 'A future for coffee?' *Journal of Applied Marketing* **6** pp. 14–17.

Referencing is a complex subject and students are advised to seek specialist help, e.g. from a library, when referencing less usual subjects.

2.12 Restatement and Repetition

1. **Restatement is used in academic writing to expand or explain:**

   a) . . . individuals and employers express great creativity in arranging alternative transport, *i.e.* private buses arranged by employers or spontaneous car sharing . . .

   b) They claim that the milk contains more omega-3 fatty acids – the polyunsaturated fatty acids which are said to prevent heart disease.

   c) . . . the contribution of cognitive ability to university success may be higher in physics and music than in sociology and psychology. *That is*, success in psychology and sociology may require abilities and dispositions not included in the entrance examination.

   In (a) and (b) the second part of the sentence explains what is meant by *alternative transport* and *omega-3 fatty acids*. In (c) the second sentence develops the first to make it clearer. Note that the restatements are introduced by i.e., a dash (–) or that is.

2. *Add a suitable restatement from the box to the following:*

   a) Higher fares for rail passengers are likely to cause a reduction in ticket sales.

   b) Two main methods of assessment are used in UK universities.

   c) 40% of the property is owned by 1% of the population.

   > *i.e. coursework and examinations.*
   >
   > *– the cost of living is expected to increase sharply.*
   >
   > *That is to say, the distribution of wealth is very unequal.*
   >
   > *In other words, this may lead to fewer people travelling by train.*

cross-reference

1.16 *Rewriting and Proof-reading*

3. *Repetition* and *redundancy* suggest that the writer is not fully in control of the material. They give the impression that either he does not properly understand the language or he is trying to 'pad' the essay by repeating the same point:

   University education in Spain is cheaper than university education in the UK.

   Homelessness is a global problem in the whole world.

   Good writing aims for economy and precision:

   University education in Spain is cheaper than in the UK.

   Homelessness is a global problem.

4. *Study the following examples of repetition and redundancy, from an essay comparing education in two countries. Underline the part that can be deleted.*

    a) Every country has a unique structure for its education system, thus it differs from country to country.

    b) Similarly China, an ancient country, has expanded its higher education.

    c) There are two differences between the UK and China in terms of higher education. Firstly, the entrance system is different in the two countries.

    d) In Spain just only 40% of students can find a job.

    e) Students who graduate from secondary schools they can send application forms to many universities.

    f) Both UK universities and Chinese universities charge fees.

    g) This essay will compare HE systems in the UK and China. Firstly, there are similar assessment methods in the UK and China.

5. **The following are common causes of repetition and redundancy.**

    Link each to one of the examples above.

    a) Repeating the same point in different words

    b) Unnecessary word – often preposition or pronoun

    c) Irrelevant comment

    d) Repetition of phrase

6. *In the following text, remove all repetition and redundancy, rewriting where necessary.*

    FAST FOOD

    Currently these days, fast food is growing in popularity. Fast food is a kind of food that people they can buy or cook quickly. This essay examines the advantages of fast food and the drawbacks of fast food. First above all, the fast food is usually tasty. Most of the people who work in offices are very busy, so that they do not have time to go to their homes for lunch. But the people who work in offices can eat tasty and delicious food in McDonald's restaurants, which are franchised in hundreds of countries. In addition, the second benefit of fast food is its cheapness. As it is produced in large quantities, this high volume means that the companies can keep costs down. As a result fast food is usually less expensive than a meal in a conventional restaurant.

2.13 Style

1. *Study the style of this paragraph and underline any examples of poor style.*

    A lot of people think that the weather is getting worse. They say that this has been going on for quite a long time. I think that they are quite right. Research has shown that we now get storms etc all the time.

2. **Academic writing attempts to be precise, semi-formal, impersonal and objective. This does not mean that pronouns like *I* and *we* are never used, but in general the focus is on presenting information as clearly and accurately as possible. In this way it differs from normal speech and writing, which is more personal and uses more lively idioms and phrases. Using these guidelines, the paragraph above can be analysed:**

A lot of people think . . .	*Imprecise – how many is 'a lot'?*
. . . the weather . . .	*Imprecise – 'weather' is short term*
. . . getting worse . . .	*Informal*
They say . . .	*Use of pronoun informal*
. . . going on . . .	*Informal phrasal verb*
. . . quite a long time.	*Imprecise – how long is this?*
I think . . .	*Informal, personal phrase*
Research . . .	*Vague – whose research?*
. . . we now get . . .	*Informal*
. . . storms etc . . .	*Vague*
. . . all the time.	*Overgeneralised*

    The paragraph can be rewritten:

    It is widely believed that the climate is deteriorating. It is claimed that this process has been continuing for nearly 100 years. This belief appears to be supported by McKinley (1997) who shows a 55% increase in the frequency of severe winter gales since 1905.

cross-reference
3.5   Caution
3.3   Adverbs
3.18 Verbs – Formality
3.20 Verbs – Passives

3. **It is difficult to give rules for academic style which apply to all subject areas. When reading books and journals in your area you should note what is acceptable. You will probably meet exceptions to the points below as you read, but if you follow these guidelines you should be able to develop a suitable style of your own.**

    a) Do not use idiomatic or colloquial vocabulary: *dad*, *guy*. Use standard English: *father*, *man*.

    b) Use vocabulary accurately. There is a difference between *rule* and *law*, or *currency* and *money*, which you are expected to know.

c) Be as precise as possible when dealing with facts or figures. Avoid phrases such as *about a hundred* or *hundreds of years ago*. If it is necessary to estimate numbers use *approximately* rather than *about*.

d) Conclusions should use tentative language. Avoid absolute statements such as *education reduces crime*. Instead use cautious phrases: *may reduce crime* or *tends to reduce crime*.

e) Avoid adverbs that show your personal attitude: *luckily, remarkably, surprisingly*.

f) Do not contract verb forms: *don't, can't*. Use the full form: *do not, cannot*.

g) Although academic English tends to use the passive more than standard English, it should not be overused. Both have their place. Compare:

> Manners (1995) claims that most companies perform worse when . . .

> It is widely agreed that most companies perform worse when . . .

In the first case, the focus is on the source, in the second on what companies do.

h) Avoid the following:

like for introducing examples. Use *such as* or *for instance*.

thing and combinations *nothing* or *something*. Use *factor, issue* or *topic*.

lots of. Use *a significant/considerable number*.

little/big. Use *small/large*.

get phrases such as *get better/worse*. Use *improve* and *deteriorate*.

good/bad are simplistic. Use *positive/negative*, e.g. *the changes had several positive aspects*

i) Do not use question forms such as *What were the reasons for the decline in wool exports?* Instead use statements: *There were four main reasons for the decline . . .*

j) Avoid numbering sections of your text, except in certain reports. Use conjunctions and signposting expressions to introduce new sections (*Turning to the question of taxation . . .*).

k) When writing lists, avoid using *etc.* or *and so on*. Insert *and* before the last item: *The forests of the twelfth century consisted of oak, ash and lime.*

l)   Avoid using two-word verbs such as *go on* or *bring up* if there is a suitable synonym. Use *continue* or *raise*.

4.   *In the following, first underline the examples of poor style and then rewrite them in a more suitable way:*

a)   Lots of people think that the railways are getting worse.

b)   Sadly, serious crime like murder is going up.

c)   You can't always trust the numbers in that report.

d)   The second thing is that most kids in that district will become criminals.

e)   I think that there's a big risk of more strikes, disorder etc.

f)   A few years ago they allowed women to vote.

g)   Regrettably, the inflation in Russia led to increased poverty, illness and so on.

h)   Some time soon they will find a vaccine for malaria.

i)   What were the main causes of the American Revolution?

5.   *Rewrite the following paragraphs in better style.*

a)   These days a lot of kids are starting school early. Years ago, they began at 5, but now it's normal to start at 4 or younger. Why is this? One thing is that mums need to get back to work. Is it good for the kids? Jenkins has studied this and says that early schooling causes social problems like stealing, drug-taking etc. I think he's right and we should pay mums to stay at home.

b) Why are there so many jams on the roads these days? One thing is that public transport like trains, buses, etc. is so dear. A long time ago cars cost a lot but now, unfortunately, they've got a lot cheaper. Another thing is that driving is a lot nicer than waiting for a bus. The trouble is that if everyone buys a car the roads get packed.

2.14 Synonyms

cross-reference

1.8   Paraphrasing

1. **When writing it is necessary to find synonyms in order to provide variety and interest for the reader:**

   > General Motors is the *largest motor company in the world*, with total revenues amounting to 15% of the *global automotive* market. *The giant firm* employs 360,000 people *internationally*.

largest company	giant firm
motor	automotive
in the world	global/internationally

   a) Synonyms are not always exactly the same in meaning, but it is important not to change the register. *Firm* is a good synonym for *company*, but *boss* is too informal to use for *manager*.

   b) Synonyms are also needed when paraphrasing or note-taking to avoid plagiarism.

2. a) The accuracy of a synonym is often dependent on context. Both *pupil* and *student* could be used to identify a 15-year-old schoolgirl, but when she goes to university only *student* is normally used. *Scholar* might be a possible synonym, but it is very formal. Similarly, at university a *lecturer* could also be called a *teacher*, but in school the only possible synonym for *teacher* is the old-fashioned *master* or *mistress*.

   b) Many basic words, e.g. *culture*, *economy*, *society* or *science*, have no effective synonyms.

cross-reference

3.2   Academic Vocabulary
3.11   Nouns – Umbrella

3. **Some common academic synonyms**

Nouns		Verbs	
goal	target	reduce	decrease
study	research	achieve	reach
results	findings	alter	change
area	field	evaluate	examine
authority	source	claim	suggest
benefit	advantage	assist	help
category	type	attach	join
component	part	challenge	question
concept	idea	clarify	explain
behaviour	conduct	quote	cite
controversy	argument	concentrate	focus

feeling	emotion	confine	limit
beliefs	ethics	show	demonstrate
expansion	increase	eliminate	remove
interpretation	explanation	found	establish
issue	topic	develop	evolve
method	system	maintain	insist
option	possibility	predict	forecast
statistics	figures	prohibit	ban
framework	structure	retain	keep
trend	tendency	strengthen	reinforce
quotation	citation	accelerate	speed up
drawback	disadvantage	reduce	cut
output	production		

4. *Find synonyms for the words and phrases in italics.*

   a) Professor Hicks *questioned* the *findings* of the *research*.

   b) The *statistics show* a steady *expansion* in applications.

   c) The institute's *prediction* has caused a major *controversy*.

   d) Cost seems to be the *leading drawback* to that *system*.

   e) They will *concentrate* on the first *option*.

   f) After the lecture she tried to *clarify* her *concept*.

   g) Three *issues* need to be *examined*.

   h) The *framework* can be *retained* but the *goal* needs to be *altered*.

   i) OPEC, the oil producers' cartel, is to *cut production* to *raise* global prices.

   j) The *trend* to smaller families has *speeded up* in the last decade.

5. *Identify the synonyms in this text by underlining them and linking them to the word they are substituting for.*

   Example: *agency – organisation*

   The chairman of the UK's food standards *agency* has said that a national advertising campaign is necessary to raise low levels of personal hygiene. The *organisation* is planning a £3m publicity programme to improve British eating habits. A survey has shown that half the population do not wash before eating, and one in five fail to wash before preparing food. There are over 6 million cases of food poisoning in this country every year, and the advertising blitz aims to cut this by 20%. This reduction, the food body believes, could be achieved by regular hand washing prior to meals.

6. *In the following text, replace all the words or phrases in italics with suitable synonyms.*

   A leading French company has started a new programme to reduce costs. The *company's programme* aims to *reduce costs* by $100 million. All staff have had pay cuts and work longer. The *company aims* to increase profits by 35% next year, and promises that *pay* for all *staff* will be *increased* if that happens.

2.15 Variation in Sentence Length

cross-reference

2.13   *Style*

1. **Short sentences are clear and easy to read:**

    > Britain is an example of the university funding problem.

    But too many short sentences are monotonous:

    > Britain is an example of the university funding problem. Fees were introduced in 1997. Spending per student had fallen by 25% since 1990. Demand continues to grow for places on the most popular courses.

    Long sentences are more interesting but can be difficult to construct and read:

    > Britain is an example of the university funding problem, since although fees were introduced in 1997 spending per student had dropped by 25% since 1990, while demand continues to grow for places on the most popular courses.

2. **Effective writing normally uses a mixture of long and short sentences.**

    Rewrite the following paragraph so that instead of six short sentences there are two long and two short sentences.

    > Worldwide, enrolments in higher education are increasing. In developed countries over half of all young people enter college. Similar trends are seen in China and South America. This growth has put financial strain on state university systems. Many countries are asking students and parents to contribute. This leads to a debate about whether students or society benefit from tertiary education.

3. *Rewrite this paragraph in fewer sentences.*

    > It is widely recognised that a university degree benefits the individual. A graduate can expect to find a better job with a higher salary. In the USA the average graduate will earn $1 million more in a lifetime than a non-graduate. Many governments now expect students to pay a proportion of tuition costs. It is argued that this discriminates against poorer students. Some countries give grants to students whose families have low incomes. Their education is seen to be beneficial for the nation as a whole.

4. *The following sentence is too long. Divide it into shorter ones.*

    > China is one developing country (but not the only one) which has imposed fees on students since 1997, but the results have been surprising: enrolments, especially in the most expensive universities, have continued to rise steeply, growing 200% overall between 1997 and 2001; it seems in this case that higher fees attract rather than

discourage students, who see them as a sign of a good education, and compete more fiercely for places, leading to the result that a place at a good college can cost $8,000 per year for fees and maintenance.

5. **It can be effective to either begin or end a paragraph with a short sentence:**

Imposing tuition fees can cause political difficulties in both developing and developed nations. In Scotland the introduction of fees, at the same time as maintenance grants were ended, led to a marked decline in enrolments from poorer students. *Fees have now been abolished in Scotland.*

Modify the following so that it has a short first or last sentence.

Developing countries are under the greatest financial pressure, and may also experience difficulties in introducing loan schemes for students, since the lack of private capital markets restricts the source of borrowing for governments, which are often unable to raise sufficient cheap funds, while a further restraint has been the high default rates by students unable to repay their loans.

6. *Write a paragraph about university funding in your country. Use a mixture of short and long sentences.*

2.16 Visual Information

cross-reference

2.9   *Numbers*

1. **Visual devices such as graphs and tables are convenient ways of displaying large quantities of information in a form that is quick and simple to understand.**

   Below are illustrations of some of the main types of visuals used in academic texts. Match the uses (a–f) to the types (1–6) and the examples (A–F) in the box below.

Uses: a) location   b) comparison   c) proportion
d) function   e) changes in time   f) statistical display

TYPES	USES	EXAMPLE
1) diagram		
2) table		
3) map		
4) pie chart		
5) bar chart		
6) line graph		

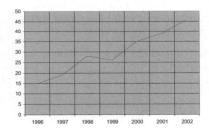

A. % students with part-time jobs

B. Part-time student enrolments

Business	205
Education	176
History	83
Law	15
Agriculture	7

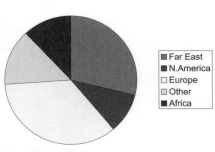

C. Origins of international students

Far East
N.America
Europe
Other
Africa

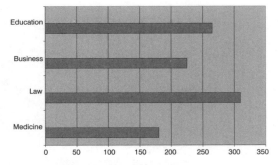

D. Student admissions by subject area

E. Structure of the Language Centre

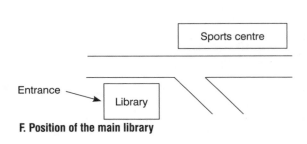

F. Position of the main library

2. **The language of change**

Verb ➝	Adverb	Verb ➘	Adjective + noun
grew	slightly	dropped	a slight drop
rose	gradually	fell	a gradual fall
increased	steadily	decreased	a sharp decrease
climbed	sharply		

Study the graph below and complete the description with phrases from the table above.

Sports centre membership a) . . . . in 1992, and then b) . . . . until 1995, reaching a peak of 4,900. It c) . . . . in 1996, but d) . . . . the next year. In 1998 there was a e) . . . ., then a peak of 6,700 in 1999, followed by a f) . . . . in 2000.

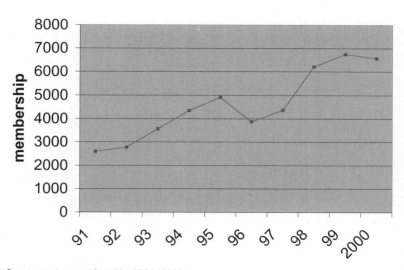

Sports centre membership 1991–2000

3. **Although visuals do largely speak for themselves, it is usual to help the reader interpret them by briefly commenting on their main features.**

The graph	shows	the changes in the price of oil since 1990
map	illustrates	the main squatter housing areas in Ankara
diagram	displays	the experimental set-up of the laboratory study

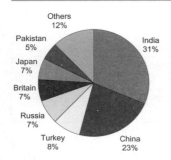

World tea consumption 1999

Read the following descriptions of the chart on the left. Which is better?

a) The chart shows the quantity of tea consumed by the world's leading tea-consuming nations. India and China together consume more than half the world's tea production, with India alone consuming about one third. Other significant tea consumers are Turkey, Russia and Britain. 'Others' includes the United States, Iran and Egypt.

b) The chart shows that 31% of the world's tea is consumed by India, 23% by China and 8% by Turkey. The fourth largest consumers are Russia, Japan and Britain, with 7% each, while Pakistan consumes 5%. Other countries account for the remaining 12%.

4. *Complete the following description of the chart below.*

The chart shows population a) . . . . in a variety of countries around the world. It b) . . . . the extreme contrast c) . . . . crowded nations such as South Korea (475 people per sq. km) and much d) . . . . countries such as Canada (3 people per sq. km). Clearly, climate plays a major e) . . . . in determining population density, f) . . . . the least crowded nations g) . . . . to have extreme climates (e.g. cold in Russia or dry in Algeria).

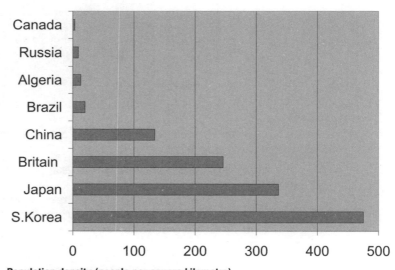

Population density (people per square kilometre)

5. *Complete the following description of the table below.*

Marriage and divorce rates (per 1,000 population)

Country	Marriage rate	Divorce rate
Britain	10.7	3.4
United States	8.6	4.7
Turkey	8.0	0.5
Iran	7.8	0.5
Japan	6.2	1.8
Russia	5.2	3.2
Spain	5.2	0.8
South Africa	4.0	0.9

The a) . . . . shows the wide variations in marriage and divorce rates in a b) . . . . of countries. The c) . . . . rate varies from 10.7 per thousand in d) . . . . to 4.0 in South Africa, while the divorce e) . . . . ranges from 4.7 in the United States to 0.5 in Turkey and f) . . . . It appears that in the United States more than g) . . . . of all marriages end in divorce, while in Turkey the h) . . . . is less than 10%. This suggests that in countries such as the United States and Britain the high marriage rate may be a i) . . . . of the high divorce rate.

6. **When referring to visual information in the text, the word** *figure* **is used for everything (such as maps, charts and graphs) except tables. Figures and tables should be numbered and given a title. Titles of tables are written above, while titles of figures are written below the data. As with other data, sources must be given for all visual information.**

Table 4: Gender balance in the School of Computing 1996–2000

	Men	Women
1996	109	34
1997	112	45
1998	125	41
1999	108	56
2000	118	72

Source: Author

If you are writing a lengthy work, such as a dissertation, you will need to provide lists of tables and figures, showing numbers, titles and page numbers, after the contents page.

7. *Complete the description of the table above.*

Table 4 shows

3. Accuracy in Writing

Student Introduction

Accuracy is only one aspect of the total fabric of good writing. Few teachers will be concerned by one minor mistake with a preposition or plural in a sentence. But if a student is making mistakes in every other word there is likely to be serious confusion about meaning, so that the teacher is unable to mark the work fairly. Many of the most common error types are highlighted in unit 1.16 *Rewriting and Proof-reading*.

Non-native users of English tend to have problems that relate to their mother tongue. Japanese speakers, for example, find it difficult to use articles in English because these are not found in Japanese. It is unrealistic for overseas students to expect to reach 100% accuracy (and many native English speakers have similar difficulty). But they should aim to steadily improve their accuracy, in order to make their work as clear and readable as possible.

The components in *Accuracy in Writing* have been chosen on the basis that they regularly cause difficulty and confusion in students' writing. These units are not intended to replace a standard grammar reference book; instead they assume a good basic knowledge of English grammar and focus on those areas of concern to the writer, rather than the speaker, of English.

As in Part 2, the units are arranged alphabetically. Students may already be aware of their weaknesses and want to focus on those, or they may seek specific assistance after getting feedback on an essay. The two tests of accuracy in the *Writing Tests* section can also be used to pinpoint weak areas.

1. **Abbreviations are an important and expanding feature of contemporary English.**

   They are used for convenience, and familiarity with abbreviations makes both academic reading and writing easier. Three main types can be found:

   a) **shortened words** – photo (photograph)

   b) **acronyms** – UNESCO

   c) **others** – NB

   a) **Shortened words** are often used without the writer being aware of the original form. *Bus* comes from *omnibus*, which is never used in modern English, but *refrigerator* is still better in written English than the informal *fridge*. *Public house* is now very formal (*pub* is acceptable), but *television* should be used instead of the idiomatic *telly*.

   b) **Acronyms** are made up of the initial letters of a name or phrase (*Aids = acquired immune deficiency syndrome*). They are read as words. The more official acronyms are written in capitals (*NATO*), but others use lower case (*nimby*). *NATO* stands for *North Atlantic Treaty Organisation*, which is a real body, while *nimby* stands for *not in my back yard*, which is a concept.

   c) **Other abbreviations** are read as sets of individual letters. They include names of countries, organisations and companies (*USA/BBC/IBM*), and also abbreviations which are only found in written English (*PTO = please turn over/ Rd = Road*). Note that in many cases such abbreviations are widely used without most users knowing the meaning of the individual letters (e.g. *DNA/DVD/ABS*).

2. **All academic subjects employ abbreviations to save time. Examples from business/economics include:**

GDP = gross domestic product	PR = public relations
PLC = public limited company	CEO = chief executive officer
IMF = International Monetary Fund	WTO = World Trade Organization

3. **There are many standard abbreviations found in some types of writing which have a full stop after them to show that it is a shortened form (*St. = saint*).**

   Other examples are *govt.* (*government*), *co.* (*company*) and *Oct.* (*October*). With type (b) and (c) abbreviations there is no standard pattern for using full stops, so both *BBC* and

B.B.C. are used. There is, however, a tendency to use full stops less. The important thing is to employ a consistent style in your work.

4.   **Abbreviations can be confusing.**

PC, for example, can mean *Police Constable* (in Britain), *personal computer* and also *politically correct*. *CD* may stand for *compact disc* or *corps diplomatique*. *PM* could be *Prime Minister* or *post meridian*. It is useful to be aware of these potential confusions.

cross-reference

1.7   Note-making

5.   a)   Certain abbreviations are found in all types of academic writing. They include:

cf. = compare

e.g. = for example

et al. = and others (used for giving names of multiple authors)

Fig. = figure (for labelling charts and graphs)

ibid. = in the same place (to refer to a source mentioned immediately before)

i.e. = that is

K = thousand

NB = take careful note

op. cit. = in the source mentioned previously

p.a. = yearly

pp. = pages

re = with reference to

b)   Other abbreviations are very subject specific and may be special to one article. In that case they need explaining:

. . . the developing countries with the highest per-capita dietary energy supplies (DES)

. . . one delegate expressed surprise that Call Centres (CCs) should . . .

6.   *Explain the abbreviations in the following sentences.*

a)   The PM told MPs that the NHS needed reform.

b)   The failure rate among IT projects reaches 70% (Smith *et al.*, 1997).

c)   The world's most populous country, i.e. China, has joined the WTO.

d)   NB CVs must be no longer than three sides of A4.

e) See the OECD's recent report on the UK.

f) The EU hopes to achieve a standard rate of VAT.

g) The CEO intends to raise spending on R&D by 40%.

h) Fig. 4. Trade patterns on the w.w.w. (1997–2001).

i) The WHO is concerned about the spread of TB.

j) Director of PR required – salary approx. $45K.

k) GM technology is leading to advances in many fields e.g. forestry.

l) Prof. Wren claimed that the quality of M.Phil. and Ph.D. research was falling.

3.2 Academic Vocabulary

cross-reference
2.14   Synonyms
3.18   Verbs – Formality
3.11   Nouns – Umbrella

1. To read and write academic texts effectively students need to be familiar with the vocabulary generally used in this context. The following are examples of some of the more common items.

Adjective	Noun	Verb
analytical	analysis	analyse
creative	creation	create
correlative	correlation	correlate
definitive	definition	define
evaluative	evaluation	evaluate
generalised	generalisation	generalise
hypothetical	hypothesis	hypothesise
indicative	indication/indicator	indicate
predictive	prediction/predictor	predict
responsive	response	respond
significant	significance	signify
synthetic	synthesis	synthesise
variable	variation/variable	vary

2. *Choose the most suitable word ending in each case.*

a) Arthur C. Clarke's pred. . . . . of earth satellites came true in 1957.

b) A signif. . . . . number of students have chosen to do that project.

c) The rate of increase var. . . . . between 5% and 8% during the period.

d) The first computer was creat. . . . . during the Second World War.

e) Scientists frequently need to ask hypoth. . . . . questions.

f) Green can be made from a synth. . . . . of blue and yellow.

g) The signif. . . . . of vitamins in diet was understood in the early twentieth century.

h) The essays were evaluat. . . . . in terms of content and accuracy.

    i)   Their research shows a strong
correl. . . . . between size and longevity.

    j)   Her anal. . . . . approach led her to
propose six types of criminals.

3.   *Complete each sentence with a suitable word from the table in (1).*

    a)   First results . . . . that this treatment
benefits patients in 70–80% of cases.

    b)   Professor Strauss wrote the . . . .
. . . . . . work on spiders in the Balkans.

    c)   Most . . . . need
to be made with care.

    d)   All the animals . . . .
to the noise by becoming agitated.

    e)   Over 3,500 questionnaires were . . . .
. . . . . . in terms of social class.

    f)   Three . . . . need to be
considered when predicting

4.   **The following adjectives are best understood and learnt as opposites:**

<table>
<tr><td>absolute</td><td>relative</td></tr>
<tr><td>abstract</td><td>concrete</td></tr>
<tr><td>logical</td><td>illogical</td></tr>
<tr><td>metaphorical</td><td>literal</td></tr>
<tr><td>precise</td><td>vague or approximate or rough</td></tr>
<tr><td>rational</td><td>irrational</td></tr>
<tr><td>relevant</td><td>irrelevant</td></tr>
<tr><td>subjective</td><td>objective</td></tr>
<tr><td>theoretical</td><td>practical or empirical or pragmatic</td></tr>
</table>

cross-reference

3.9   Nouns and Adjectives

Faith, hope and charity are all *abstract* concepts.

The *metaphorical* use of the word 'key' is probably more common than its *literal* one.

The study of statistics is highly *relevant* to economics.

Her study of women's social position was criticised for being too *subjective.*

In Europe, *empirical* research began in the sixteenth century.

5. *Complete each sentence with a suitable adjective from the table in (4).*

a) The . . . . number killed in the war will never be known.

b) His . . . . approach led him to ignore some inconvenient facts.

c) Many . . . . ideas, such as astrology, are still popular.

d) It is sufficient to give . . . . figures for national populations.

e) Only after 200 years could an . . . . biography be written.

f) Although he was a qualified dentist it was . . . . to his new job as a priest.

g) Cathedrals are a . . . . example of religious faith.

3.3 Adverbs

1. **Adverbs are used in academic texts in a variety of ways. Among the most important are:**

   a) to provide more detail, with verbs and adjectives:

   Reasonably good data are available for only . . .

   . . . decomposition *eventually* ceases in modern landfills . . .

   b) individually, often at the beginning of sentences, to introduce new points:

   Currently, the earth's atmosphere appears to be . . .

   Alternatively, the use of non-conventional renewable energies . . .

   (These can be similar in function to conjunctions.)

2. **Adverbs linked to verbs and adjectives usually fall into three groups.**

   a) Time (when?)

   previously published

   retrospectively examined

   b) Degree (how much?)

   declined *considerably*

   contribute *substantially*

   c) Manner (in what way?)

   medically complicated

   remotely located

cross-reference

2.13   *Style*

3. **Adverbs used individually need to be employed with care. It is dangerous to overuse them, since they are often like the author's 'voice', commenting on the topic. As the academic writer aims to be objective, adverbs like *fortunately* or *remarkably* may be unsuitable. However, other, less subjective adverbs can be useful for opening paragraphs or linking ideas. The following examples are often followed by a comma.**

Time	Relating ideas
recently	*clearly*
increasingly	*obviously*
originally	*(not) surprisingly*
presently	*alternatively*
currently	*similarly*
traditionally	*(more) importantly*

4. *Insert a suitable adverb from the table into the gaps in the sentences.*

    a) Most houses do not have electricity. . . . ., then, there is little chance of improving living standards.

    b) . . . ., the internet was mainly used for academic purposes.

    c) Some courses are assessed purely by exams. . . . ., coursework may be employed.

    d) . . . ., there has been growing concern about financing the health service.

    e) Many birds use bright colours to attract a mate. . . . ., flowers advertise their position to fertilising insects.

    f) . . . ., the development should be acceptable environmentally.

cross-reference

2.16   Visual Information

5. **The following adverbs are used to describe changes in the rate of something:**

small	medium	large
gradually	substantially	quickly
slightly	significantly	sharply
marginally	steadily	dramatically
slowly	considerably	rapidly

Note that certain adverbs are mainly used to describe changes in time:

Production in Russia rose *slowly* from 1920 to 1929. (a little every year)

Others are commonly used to show changes in amount:

The birth rate increased *slightly* after the revolution. (by a small quantity)

The most suitable adverb depends on what is being discussed. For example,

Over the period, the inflation rate fell *significantly* from 6% to 4.5%.

In 2004, sales dropped *slightly*, by 1.5%.

cross-reference

2.9   Numbers

6. *Use a suitable adverb to complete the following sentences.*

    a) Last year inflation increased . . . . from 2% to 2.3%.

    b) Life expectancy has risen . . . . in the last 20 years, by about 15%.

c)   The price was reduced . . . ., so that a £12 book
      was offered for £6.

d)   Sales rose . . . . while he was chairman,
      averaging 14% per year.

e)   The numbers of people voting has declined . . . .,
      from 80% to 65%.

f)   The crime rate climbed . . . . in the early 1990s,
      by 20–25% a year.

g)   In the last four years unemployment has fallen. . . . .,
      from 5% to 2.5%.

h)   In the first two years of the war the suicide rate dropped
      . . . ., by over 30% each year.

3.4 Articles

cross-reference

3.10 Nouns – Countable and
Uncountable

1. **Unless they are uncountable, all nouns need an article when used in the singular. The article can be either *a/an* or *the*. Compare:**

   a) Research is an important activity in universities.

   b) *The* research begun by Dr Mathews was continued by Professor Brankovic.

   c) *A* survey was conducted among 200 patients in the clinic.

   In (a) *research*, which is usually uncountable, is being used in a general sense.

   In (b) a specific piece of research is identified.

   In (c) the survey is being mentioned for the first time.

2. **The rules for using *the* (the definite article) are quite complex.**

   Decide why it is used, or not, in the following examples.

   a) The most famous fictional detective is Sherlock Holmes.

   b) The USA was founded in the eighteenth century.

   c) The government changed its attitude in the 1980s.

   d) In many companies, the knowledge of most employees is a wasted resource.

   e) The moon orbits the earth every 28 days.

   f) The south is characterised by poverty and emigration.

   g) Charles Dickens, the English novelist, died in 1870.

   h) The River Trent runs through the middle of England.

   i) The World Health Organization was founded in 1948.

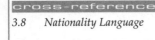

cross-reference

3.8 Nationality Language

3. **In general, *the* is used with:**

   a) superlatives (*most famous*)

   b) time periods (*eighteenth century/1980s*)

   c) unique things (*government/moon/earth*)

   d) specified things (*knowledge of most employees*)

   e) regions and rivers (*south/River Trent*)

   f) very well-known people and things (*English novelist*)

   g) institutions and bodies (*World Health Organization*)

   h) positions (*middle*)

   It is *not* used with:

i) names of countries, except for the UK, the USA and a few others

j) abstract nouns (*poverty*)

k) companies/bodies named after people/places, e.g. Sainsbury's, Sheffield University

4. *In the following sentences, decide if the words underlined are specific or not. Insert* **the** *if specific.*

Example:

. . . . inflation was the greatest problem for . . . . . . Brazilian government.

Inflation was the greatest problem for *the* Brazilian government.

a) . . . . engineering is the main industry in this region.

b) . . . . moons of Jupiter were discovered in . . . . eighteenth century.

c) . . . . global warming is partly caused by . . . . fossil fuels.

d) . . . . Russian revolution was largely a result of . . . . First World War.

e) . . . . fraud is costing . . . . banking industry millions of pounds a year.

f) . . . . drought may have been a factor in . . . . decline of the Maya empire.

g) . . . . forests of Scandinavia produce most of . . . . world's paper.

h) . . . . French police have issued a warning about . . . . terrorist groups.

i) . . . . computer crime has grown by 200% in . . . . last decade.

j) . . . . Japanese emperor lives in . . . . centre of Tokyo.

k) Already 3% of . . . . US working population are employed in . . . . call centres.

l) . . . . purpose of this paper is to evaluate . . . . intelligence tests.

m) Picasso, ... Spanish painter, was born in . . . . nineteenth century.

n) . . . . best definition is often . . . . simplest.

5.   *Complete the following text by inserting* **a/an/the** *(or nothing) in each gap.*

THE ORIGINS OF @

Giorio Stabile, a). . . . . . . professor of b). . . . . . . history at La Sapienza university in Rome, has demonstrated that c). . . . . . . @ sign, now used in email addresses, was actually invented 500 years ago. Professor Stabile has shown that d). . . . . . . @, now e). . . . . . . symbol of f). . . . . . . internet, was first used by Italian merchants during g). . . . . . . sixteenth century.

He claims that it originally represented h). . . . . . . unit of volume, based on i). . . . . . . large jars used to carry liquids in j). . . . . . . ancient Mediterranean world. He has found k). . . . . . . first example of its use in l). . . . . . . letter written in 1546 by m). . . . . . . merchant from Florence. n). . . . . . . letter, which was sent to Rome, announces o). . . . . . . arrival in p). . . . . . . Spain of ships carrying gold from South America.

q). . . . . . . professor argues that r). . . . . . . @ sign derives from s). . . . . special script used by these merchants, which was developed in t). . . . . . . sixteenth century. According to him, u). . . . . . . loop around v). . . . . . . 'a' is typical of that style. He found w). . . . . . . evidence while researching x). . . . . . . visual history of y). . . . . twentieth century.

3.5   Caution

2.13   *Style*

1.   **A cautious style is necessary in many areas of academic writing:**

> Primary products . . . *usually* have low supply and demand elasticities . . .

> . . . multiple factors *may* lead to a psychiatric consultation

> . . . some parameters *might* depend on the degree of water content in the sand

> . . . women *tend to* value privacy more than men

> . . . other studies *suggest* that some permanent modal shift will occur

> Areas where caution is particularly important include:

a)   outlining a hypothesis which needs to be tested (e.g. in an introduction)

b)   discussing the results of a study, which may not be conclusive

c)   commenting on the work of other writers

2.8   *Generalisations*
3.19   *Verbs – Modal*

2.   **Caution is needed to avoid making statements which are too simplistic:**

> Poor education leads to crime.

> Such statements are rarely completely true. There is usually an exception which needs to be considered. Caution can be shown in several ways:

> | (modal verb) | Poor education *can* lead to crime. |
> | (adverb) | Poor education *frequently* leads to crime. |
> | (verb/phrase) | Poor education *tends to* lead to crime. |
> | | *There is a tendency* for poor education to lead to crime. |

Complete the box below with more examples.

Modals	Adverbs	Verb/phrase
can	frequently	tends to
		there is a tendency

3.   *Rewrite the following sentences in a more cautious way.*

   a)   Private companies are more efficient than state-owned businesses.

   b)   Computer manuals are difficult to understand.

   c)   Older students perform better at university than younger ones.

   d)   Exploring space is a waste of valuable resources.

   e)   English pronunciation is confusing.

   f)   Global warming will cause the sea level to rise.

   g)   Science students work harder than those studying humanities.

   h)   Concrete is the best material for building bridges.

4.   **Another way to express caution is to use** *quite, rather* **or** *fairly* **before an adjective.**

   a *fairly* accurate summary

   quite a significant correlation

   a *rather* inconvenient location

   NB *Quite* is often used before the article. It is generally used positively, while *rather* tends to be used negatively.

Insert **quite/rather/fairly** *in the following to emphasise caution.*

   a)   Charles was an insignificant king who reigned for only 3 years.

   b)   The survey was a comprehensive study of student opinion.

   c)   His second book had a hostile reception.

   d)   The latest type of arthritis drugs are expensive.

   e)   The first-year students were fascinated by her lectures.

3.22   *Verbs of Reference*

5.   **When referring to sources, the verb used indicates the degree of caution appropriate. Compare:**

Widmerpool (1999) *states* that junior doctors work longer than . . . (positive)

Le Bas (1983) *suggests* that more training would result in . . . (cautious)

Other verbs which imply tentative or cautious findings are:

think/consider/hypothesise/believe/claim/presume

6.   *Rewrite the following text in more cautious language.*

A team of American scientists have found a way to reverse the ageing process. They fed diet supplements, found in health food shops, to elderly rats, which were then tested for memory and stamina. The animals displayed more active behaviour after taking the supplements, and their memory improved. In addition, their appearance became more youthful and their appetite increased.

The researchers say that this experiment is a clear indication of how the problems of old age can be overcome. They state that in a few years' time everyone will be able to look forward to a long and active retirement.

1. *Study the following sentences.*

    The storm *affected* large parts of northern France.

    An immediate *effect* of the price rise was a fall in demand.

    Affect and *effect* are different words which are often
    confused because they have similar spellings and
    meanings. However, *affect* is a verb, while *effect* is
    commonly used as a noun.

    Study the differences between other similar confusing pairs
    (most common use in brackets).

accept (verb)/except (prep.)
It is difficult to accept their findings.
The report is finished except for the conclusion.

close (adj.)/close (verb)
The town was built close to the gold mines.
The library will be closed all weekend.

compliment (noun/verb)/complement (verb)
Her colleagues complimented her on her presentation.
His latest book complements his previous research on neurotic behaviour.

economic (adj.)/economical (adj.)
Sharing a car to work was an economical move.
Inflation was one economic result of the war.

its (pronoun)/it's (pronoun + verb)
It's widely agreed that smoking is dangerous.
The car's advanced design was its most distinct feature.

lose (verb)/loose (adj.)
No general ever plans to lose a battle.
He stressed the loose connection between religion and psychology.

past (noun/adj./prep.)/passed (verb)
Demand has been growing for the past five years.
The resolution was passed by 12 votes to 7.

principal (adj./noun)/principle (noun)
Zurich is the principal city of Switzerland.
All economists recognise the principle of supply and demand.

rise (verb – past tense rose)/raise (verb – past tense raised)
The population of London rose by 35% in the century.
The university raised its fees by 10% last year.

> **quite (adv.)/quiet (noun/adj.)**
>
> It was quite difficult to explain her hypothesis.
>
> Everyone needs a quiet environment to work effectively.
>
> **site (noun)/sight (noun)**
>
> The site of the battle is now covered by an airport.
>
> His sight began to weaken when he was in his eighties.
>
> **tend to (verb)/trend (noun)**
>
> Young children tend to enjoy making a noise.
>
> In many countries there is a trend towards smaller families.

2. *Choose the correct word in each sentence.*

   a) His conclusions were *quiet/quite* interesting, but controversial.

   b) Millions of people are attempting to *lose/loose* weight.

   c) Sunspots have been known to *affect/effect* radio communication.

   d) Professor Poledna received their *compliments/complements* politely.

   e) The ancient symbol depicted a snake eating *it's/its* tail.

   f) Both social and *economical/economic* criteria need to be examined.

   g) It took many years for some of Freud's theories to be *accepted/excepted*.

3. *Some of the following contain mistakes. Find and correct them.*

   a) The past has been described as like 'a foreign country.'

   b) One of the most famous sights in Paris is the Eiffel Tower.

   c) Re-using old envelopes was one economic suggestion.

   d) He was a man of strict principals, who never borrowed any money.

   e) Accept for two students they all spoke Arabic.

   f) The taste of lemon complemented the rich flavour of the fish.

   g) Only seven out of a class of sixteen passed the exam.

   h) Most oil companies plan to rise prices in the new year.

3.7 Conjunctions

1. **Conjunctions are words and phrases such as *and* or *but* which join parts of a sentence together. There are six main types of conjunctions:**

   a) **addition**   *Furthermore,* child mortality rates must be examined.

   b) **result**   Prices are rising worldwide, *thus* encouraging investment.

   c) **reason**   *Due to* the strike today's classes are cancelled.

   d) **time**   *Thirdly,* the role of the architect will be reviewed.

   e) **example**   Various writers have examined the issue, *for instance* Van Exel (2000).

   f) **opposition**   *Although* this study concentrates mainly on peak-time travellers . . .

2. *Decide which type (a–f) the following sentences belong to.*

   a) Before the Roman invasion the economy was mainly agricultural.   (   )

   b) The results were checked because they were so surprising.   (   )

   c) Estimates suggest that the effects will continue, but at a more moderate rate.   (   )

   d) Some Asian economies, for example Indonesia, are growing more slowly.   (   )

   e) Moreover, travel information is very important for route planning.   (   )

   f) The findings were ambiguous, therefore the study was revised.   (   )

   g) The deadline is next week, so speed is vital.   (   )

   h) There is a serious problem in the district, namely unemployment.   (   )

3. **Conjunctions act as signposts for the reader, giving the main meaning of the phrase they introduce:**

Addition	✚
Result	⇨
Reason	⇦
Time	⧗
Example	↳
Opposition	⊘

Study the use of conjunctions in signposting the following paragraph.

The Brazilian coast was hit by a strange storm in March 2004. It moved inland at speeds of over 150 k.p.h. ✚ *and* caused considerable damage. Named Catarina, this storm behaved like a hurricane ◊ *but* could not have been one. This was ⇐ *because* hurricanes do not occur in the South Atlantic. ◊ *However*, Catarina was not an ordinary tropical storm ⇐ *since* it had a hurricane 'eye' and was of hurricane strength. ⧗ *After* checking their records, meteorologists decided that Catarina really was a hurricane, the first ever recorded in the region. Their research suggests that sea temperatures are rising rapidly, ⇨ *thereby* developing enough energy to cause hurricanes.

4. *Underline the conjunctions in the following text and draw the 'signposts'.*

Many Asian students chose the college because of its

excellent reputation. Kim, for example, liked the spacious

campus. He is self-funded and pays a tuition fee of £9,500

per year. But many students find language a barrier, so

that they only socialise with other overseas students,

while others complain about the college facilities. Firstly,

accommodation is said to be noisy and inconvenient, and

furthermore the library is seen as poorly equipped.

5. *Complete the table to show as many examples of conjunctions as possible.*

Addition	Result	Reason	Time	Example	Opposition
furthermore					

6. *Insert a suitable conjunction in each gap.*

a) . . . . the course was voluntary, most students attended.

b) The longest day of the year, ... June 21st, was a time of festivity.

c) . . . . checking the equipment the experiment was repeated.

d) . . . . most people use the train, a minority walk or cycle.

e) Brick is a thermally efficient building material. It is, ..., cheap.

f) Demand has increased for summer courses, ... extra ones are offered this year.

g) Many writers, ... Chekhov, have been doctors.

h) . . . . the increase in residence fees more students are moving out.

i) The first stage was to write a clear questionnaire. . . . . 200 people were interviewed.

j) . . . . Mustafa was in the lecture his car was being repaired.

7. *Complete the following biography by inserting suitable conjunctions.*

THE BEATLES

The group which became the Beatles was formed in 1960 by John Lennon and Paul McCartney, with George Harrison and Ringo Starr joining later. a). . . . . playing in small clubs for 2 years their first record, *Love Me Do,* was released. *She Loves You*, in 1963, broke all previous sales records in Britain. b). . . . . their simplicity, the early Beatles songs c). . . . . *Yesterday* and *Paperback Writer* are still seen as masterpieces of musical genius. d). . . . ., the unusual haircuts and clothes worn by the Beatles fitted well with the style of the mid-1960s. The popularity of the group soon spread to the USA and e). . . . . around the world, f). . . . . the media invented the term 'Beatlemania' to describe the excitement that was part of their tours. g). . . . . their popularity the group were awarded the MBE by the Queen in 1965, h). . . . . this caused anger among some of the older holders of this award.

In 1966 the Beatles stopped live performances, i). . . . . their music was becoming too complex to produce on stage. A year later *Sgt. Pepper's Lonely Hearts Club Band* was released, j). . . . . .was immediately recognised as one of the most influential works in the history of popular music. k). . . . ., the pressures of fame were beginning to affect all the members of the band, l). . . . . that they found it harder to work together. They played together for the last time in 1969 and m). . . . . split up in 1970.

8. **Conjunctions of opposition**

   Note the position of the conjunctions in the following examples.

   The economy is strong, *but/yet* there are frequent strikes.

   Although/while there are frequent strikes, the economy is strong.

   In spite of/despite the frequent strikes, the economy is strong.

   There are frequent strikes. *However/nevertheless*, the economy is strong.

   Write two sentences in each case.

   Example: The equipment was expensive/unreliable.

   The equipment was expensive but unreliable.

   Although the equipment was expensive it was unreliable.

   a) The government claimed that inflation was falling. The opposition said it was rising.

      i)

      ii)

   b) This department must reduce expenditure. It needs to install new computers.

      i)

      ii)

9. *Finish the sentences in a suitable way.*

   a) In contrast to America, where gun ownership is common,

   b) Despite leaving school at the age of 14

   c) The majority displayed a positive attitude to the proposal, but

   d) While the tutor insisted that the essay was easy,

   e) Although the spring was cold and dry

3.8 Nationality Language

1. **Most nationalities have a regular pattern of nouns and adjectives.**

    Germany is a leading industrial economy.   (country)

    The *German* capital is Berlin.   (adjective)

    German is spoken by over 100 million.   (language)

    Germans/The Germans like wine.   (people)

    (Most national adjectives end in *-an/-ian/-ish/-ch/-ese/-i*.)

2. **Some nationalities are less regular.**

    Holland/The Netherlands is located between Belgium and Germany.

    The *Dutch* capital is The Hague.

    Dutch is related to German.

    Dutch people often speak English well.

Country	People	Country	People	Country	People
Denmark	Danes	Iraq	Iraqis	Switzerland	Swiss
Greece	Greeks	Pakistan	Pakistanis	Chile	Chileans
Poland	Poles	Thailand	Thais	Portugal	Portuguese

3. *Write similar sentences to those above about **two** of the countries below:*

France	Japan	Egypt	India	Ireland	Mexico

i)   i)

ii)   ii)

iii)   iii)

iv)   iv)

cross-reference

3.4   Articles

4. **The definite article is used with a few countries:**

    The United Arab Emirates   The United States

    The United Kingdom   The Czech Republic

    With national adjectives ending in *-an/-ian* it is possible to say:

    Italians/The Italians/Italian people have enjoyed opera for over 200 years.

With other endings the first form is not possible:

The Japanese/Japanese people like watching sumo wrestling.

NB *England* is not a political unit. Although it is possible to use *English people/English food* the nationality is *British*. The country's name is *Britain* or the *United Kingdom*.

5.   *Complete the spaces in the following sentences with* **one** *word.*

a)   Beijing is the . . . . capital.

b)   The rouble is the . . . . currency.

c)   The largest city in . . . . is Sydney.

d)   Many . . . . people enjoy going to bullfights.

e)   Bill Clinton was the . . . . president.

f)   . . . . are the only South Americans who speak Portuguese.

g)   The . . . . capital is Baghdad.

h)   . . . . speak Spanish and make fine cigars.

6.   *Write sentences about some of the people in the box, giving their nationality.*

Ronaldo	Bill Gates	Pablo Picasso	Bob Marley
Kofi Annan	Mao Tse-tung	Akio Morita	Beethoven
Nelson Mandela	Josef Stalin	Mahatma Gandhi	Yasser Arafat

Example: Ronaldo is a Brazilian footballer/Ronaldo comes from Brazil.

a)

b)

c)

d)

e)

f)

g)

h)

3.9   Nouns and Adjectives

cross-reference	
3.2	*Academic Vocabulary*
3.6	*Confusing Pairs*

1. **Compare these sentences:**

    The *efficiency* of the machine depends on the *precision* of its construction.

    Precise construction results in an *efficient* machine.

    The first sentence uses the nouns *efficiency* and *precision*. The second uses adjectives: *precise* and *efficient*. Although the meaning is similar the first sentence is more formal. Effective academic writing requires accurate use of both, which can be easily confused.

2. *Underline and correct the mistakes in the following:*

    a) Some areas of the capital are not safety.

    b) Various culture patterns in French society need to be considered.

    c) The deep of the lake is calculated at 550 metres.

    d) A health diet includes fresh fruit and vegetables.

3. *Complete the gaps in the table below.*

Noun	Adjective	Noun	Adjective	Noun	Adjective
height		reliability		heat	
	strong		confident		true
width		probability		necessity	
	long		dangerous		relevant

4. *Insert a suitable noun or adjective from the table in each sentence.*

    a) The building's . . . . is due to its massive steel frame.

    b) The . . . . of the matter may never be known since all the records are lost.

    c) There is a strong . . . . that coffee prices will fall next year.

    d) In some places the River Zambesi is more than 3 kilometres . . . .

    e) The results are so surprising it will be . . . . to repeat the experiment.

    f) It is not easy to see the . . . . of art history to engineering.

    g) Regularly backing up computer files reduces the . . . . of losing vital work.

    h) Revising for exams is a tedious . . . .

i) This data appears to be . . . . and should not be trusted.

j) . . . . in the banking system was destroyed by years of inflation.

5. *Underline the adjective(s) in each sentence and write the related noun(s) in brackets.*

Example:

Few patients are <u>likely</u> to suffer side-effects from the drug. (likelihood)

a) Various methods of dealing with the spread of malaria were suggested.   (   )

b) Dr Lee adopted an analytical approach to the inquiry.
                                                                 (   )

c) Antibiotics were not available in the first half of the twentieth century.   (   )

d) Her major contribution to the research was her study of folklore in Spain.   (   )

e) The precise number of people affected by the earthquake is unknown.   (   ) (   )

f) Some progress was made in the theoretical area. (   )

g) A frequent complaint is that too much work is expected in the first semester.   (   )

h) We took a more critical approach to irrigation.   (   )

i) The Department of Social Policy is offering three courses this year.   (   )

j) Finally, the practical implications of my findings will be examined.   (   )

6. *Complete the gaps in the table below.*

Noun	Adjective	Noun	Adjective
approximation	approximate		particular
superiority		reason	
	strategic		synthetic
politics		economy	
	industrial		cultural
exterior		average	

7. *Complete the sentences with nouns or adjectives from the table above.*

a) The . . . . consequences of the war were inflation and unemployment.

b) 365.25 days is an . . . . of the length of the solar year.

c) One . . . . of British weather is that it is very changeable.

d) All . . . . doors are fitted with security systems.

e) They attempted to make a . . . . of all the different proposals.

f) The . . . . length of time patients have to wait is 34.6 weeks.

g) The traditional idea that the sun went round the earth was . . . ., but wrong.

h) Ancient Japanese . . . . was highly developed in areas such as poetry and ceramics.

3.10 Nouns – Countable and Uncountable

1. **Most nouns in English are countable, but the following are generally uncountable, i.e. they are not usually used with numbers or the plural '-s'.**

accommodation	information	scenery
advice	knowledge	staff
behaviour	money	traffic
commerce	news	travel
data	permission	trouble
education	progress	vocabulary
equipment	research	weather
furniture	rubbish	work

3.16   *Singular or Plural?*

2. **Another group of uncountable nouns is used for materials:**

    wood/rubber/iron/coffee/paper/water/oil/stone

    Little *wood* is used in the construction of motor vehicles.

    Huge amounts of *paper* are used to produce magazines.

    Many of these nouns can be used as countable nouns with a rather different meaning:

    Over twenty daily *papers* are published in Delhi.

    Most *woods* are home to a wide variety of birds.

3. **The most difficult group can be used as either countable or uncountable nouns, often with quite different meanings (further examples: *business/capital/experience*).**

    She developed *an interest* in bio-genetics.

    The bank is paying 4% *interest* on 6-month deposits.

    Other nouns with a similar pattern are used for general concepts (*love/fear/hope*).

    Most people feel that *life* is too short. (in general)

    Nearly twenty *lives* were lost in the mining accident. (in particular)

4. **Note the importance of the type of noun in the following structures:**

    QUESTIONS   *How much accommodation* (U) is available for rent?

    How many rooms (C) are vacant next month?

NEGATIVES   *Not much/Little equipment* (U) was needed for the experiment.

Not many/Few machines (C) were functioning in the IT room.

Complete the following sentences to show the differences in meaning.

a) Three years' work experience . . . .

b) She had some exciting experiences while. . . . .

c) Most small businesses have . . . .

d) In many countries it is normal to discuss business . . . .

e) A number of capitals such as Washington and Canberra are . . . .

f) Huge amounts of capital are needed . . . .

g) Two world wars in 30 years caused . . . .

h) War is a feature of . . . .

i) . . . . was the cause of six deaths.

j) Death is . . . .

k) New medicines are being developed . . . .

l) Studying medicine at university can be . . . .

5. *In the following sentences, choose the correct alternative.*

a) *Little/few* news reached the prisoners in the castle.

b) He established three successful *businesses/business* in 1995.

c) Substantial *experiences/experience* of report writing *are/is* required.

d) It has often been claimed that *travel broadens/travels broaden* the mind.

e) *Paper was/papers were* very expensive in the twelfth century.

f) How *much advice/many advices* were they given before coming to Britain?

g) She had *little interest/few interests* outside her work.

h) The insurance policy excludes the effects of civil *war/wars*.

i) *Irons were/iron was* first powered by electricity in the twentieth century.

j) They studied the *behaviour/behaviours* of three groups of lions over 2 years.

6. *Complete the gaps in the following paragraph with* **much/many/little/few.**

Very a). . . . . data is available to students of

housing of the sixth to ninth centuries AD. No complete

examples survive, and researchers are not certain how

b). . . . . information can be taken from the

literature. It is not clear how c). . . . . people

lived in each house, and in the d). . . . . sites that

have been investigated (only four in the whole country)

e). . . . . progress has been made towards finding

a standard floor plan.

3.11 Nouns – Umbrella

cross-reference

3.2   *Academic Vocabulary*

1. **A range of 'umbrella' nouns is used to express basic ideas in academic writing:**

    Molecular biology is an interesting new *field*.

    The *concept* of class was first discussed in the eighteenth century.

    Freud developed a new *approach* in his second book.

    They are rather formal and need to be used accurately.

    Read the following and find a synonym for each word in italics from the box below.

    a) The second *factor* in the accident was the cold weather.

    b) Harvey's *concept* of the circulation of the blood was first presented in 1628.

    c) Snow is a rare *phenomenon* in Rome.

    d) The President's resignation gave a new *aspect* to the national crisis.

    e) A barcode scanner is a *device* used at supermarket checkouts.

    f) Her *field* is the history of life insurance.

    g) The National Institute for Clinical Excellence is a *body* created to assess medical drugs.

    h) Mendel's work on genetics provided new *perspectives* for biologists.

    i) Their main *concern* is to prevent pollution in rivers and lakes.

    j) Their new *system* allows errors to be detected in 12 seconds.

    k) The survey identified three *categories* of bus user.

    l) The most serious *issue* raised at the meeting was student accommodation.

process	organisation	machine		theory
event	types	consideration	area	
views				feature
	cause		problem	

2. *Insert a suitable umbrella noun in the following sentences.*

    a) The Students' Union is a . . . . designed to promote students' interests.

    b) Rainbows are a common natural . . . .

    c) Completion of the new building was delayed by safety . . . .

    d) Environmental law is an increasingly popular . . . .

    e) In 1956 he patented a . . . . for measuring the height of waves.

    f) Jung's . . . . of the 'anima' has been strongly criticised.

    g) His paper examined three . . . . of the problem of tissue rejection.

    h) Three . . . . of father were identified; 'involved', 'semi-detached' and 'disengaged'.

    i) The main . . . . discussed was lack of support from tutors.

    j) One . . . . in the collapse of the business was the rise in oil prices.

    k) The discovery of DNA created fresh . . . . in medicine.

3. Keep a record of other umbrella nouns you meet.

Umbrella noun	Synonym

3.12 Prefixes and Suffixes

1. *Automatically* and *uncontrollable* are examples of words containing prefixes and suffixes. Words like these are much easier to understand if you know how prefixes and suffixes affect word meaning.

   Prefixes change or give the meaning.

   Suffixes show the meaning or the word class.

   The machine started *automatically*.

   The class of young boys was *uncontrollable*.

Prefix	Meaning	Suffix	Word class/ meaning
auto-	by itself	-ally	adverb
un-	negative	-able	ability

2. **Prefixes**

   a) Negative prefixes. *un-*, *in-*, *mis-* and *dis-* often give adjectives and verbs a negative meaning: *un*clear, *in*sane, *mis*hear, *dis*agree

   b) A wide variety of prefixes define meaning, e.g. *pre-* usually means 'before', hence *pre*fer, *pre*history and, of course, *pre*fix!

3. **Common prefixes of meaning**

   Find the meaning(s) of each prefix. (NB Some prefixes have more than one meaning.)

auto	autopilot	The plane flew on *autopilot* for six hours.
co	co-ordinator	The *co-ordinator* invited them to a meeting.
ex	ex-girlfriend	He met his *ex-girlfriend* at the station.
ex	exclusive	It is difficult to join such an *exclusive* club.
micro	microscope	She studied the tiny animals with a *microscope*.
multi	multinational	Ford is a *multinational* motor company.
over	oversleep	After *oversleeping* twice she got an alarm clock.
post	postpone	The meeting is *postponed* to next Monday.
re	return	*Return* the letter to the sender.

sub	subtitle	Chinese films have *subtitles* in Britain.
under	undergraduate	Most *undergraduate* courses last 3 years.
under	undercook	*Undercooked* meat can be a health hazard.

4. *Prefixes allow new words to be created. Suggest possible meanings for the recently developed words in italics.*

a) Criminal activity seems to be very common among the *underclass*.

b) The passengers found the jet was *overbooked* and had to wait for the next flight.

c) The *microclimate* in my garden means that I can grow early tomatoes.

d) It is claimed that computers have created a *post-industrial* economy.

e) Most film stars have *ex-directory* phone numbers.

f) The class was *underwhelmed* by the quality of the lecture.

5. **Suffixes**

a) Some suffixes like *-ion, -ive* or *-ly* help the reader find the word class, e.g. noun, verb or adjective.

b) Other suffixes add to meaning, e.g. *-ful* or *-less* after an adjective have a positive or negative effect (thought*ful*/ thought*less*).

6. **Word class suffixes**

Nouns	-er often indicates a person: teacher, gardener
	-ee can show the person who is the subject: employee, trainee
	-ism and -ist are used with belief systems and their supporters: socialism/socialist
	-ness converts an adjective into a noun: sad/ sadness
	-ion changes a verb to a noun: convert/conversion
Adjectives	-ive: effective, constructive
	-al: commercial, agricultural
	-ous: precious, serious
Verbs	-ise/-ize to form verbs from adjectives: private/ privatise
Adverbs	-ly: most (but not all) adverbs have this suffix: happily

7. **Meaning suffixes**

A few suffixes contribute to the meaning of the word:

-able has the meaning of 'ability': a *watchable* film, *changeable* weather

-wards means 'in the direction of': the ship sailed *northwards*

-ful and *-less*: *hopeful* news, a *leaderless* army

8. *Give the word class and suggest possible meanings for:*

   a) cancellation   f) unpredictable

   b) coincidental   g) saleable

   c) uncooperatively   h) interviewee

   d) evolutionary   i) surrealism

   e) protester   j) symbolically

9. *Study each sentence and find the meanings of the words in italics.*

   a) The film is a French–Italian *co-production* made by a *subsidiary* company.

   b) When the car crashed she screamed *involuntarily* but was *unharmed*.

   c) Using *rechargeable* batteries has *undoubted* benefits for the environment.

   d) The *unavailability* of the product is due to the *exceptional* weather.

   e) There is a *theoretical* possibility of the cloth *disintegrating*.

3.13 Prepositions

cross-reference

3.21   Verbs and Prepositions

1. **Underline the prepositions in the following text.**

    The purpose of this paper is to examine the development of the textile industry in Britain over the period 1750–1850. This clearly contributed to the nation's industrialisation, and was valuable for stimulating exports. In conclusion, the paper sets out to demonstrate the relationship between the decline in agricultural employment and the supply of cheap labour in the factory context.

    The table lists the main ways of using prepositions. **Find one example of each in the text.**

Noun + preposition	*purpose of*
Verb + preposition	
Adjective + preposition	
Phrasal verb	
Preposition of place	
Preposition of time	
Phrase	

    NB the difference between phrasal verbs and verbs with prepositions:

    The cars are *made in* Korea. (verb + preposition = easy to understand)

    The writer *made up* the story in a night. (phrasal verb = hard to understand)

2. *Study these further examples of preposition use and decide on their type.*

    a) There are a number *of* limitations to be considered . . .   (noun +)

    b) The results would be applicable *to* all managers . . .(   )

    c) . . . the data was gathered *from* a questionnaire   (   )

    d) All the items were placed *within* their categories   (   )

    e) The results *of* the investigation are still pertinent . . .
                                                                                (   )

    f) The respondents had spent *on* average 4.9 years . . .
                                                                                (   )

g) ... most countries *in* sub-Saharan Africa ...   (   )

h) ... *within* a short spell of four years   (   )

3. *Insert a suitable preposition before or after the nouns in the sentences below.*

a) Evidence is presented in support . . . . . the value of women's work.

b) A small change . . . . . demand can lead to large price rises.

c) Many examples . . . . . high levels of calcium were found.

d) No cure . . . . . malaria has yet been found.

e) We tried to assess the feasibility . . . . . allowing children to choose their own subjects.

f) The second point is their impact . . . . . developing countries.

4. *Complete the following phrases with the correct prepositions.*

a) . . . . the whole   e) in support . . .

b) point . . . . . view   f) . . . . . the other hand

c) in respect . . . . . .   g) . . . . . order to

d) . . . . . spite of   h) standard . . . . . living

5. *Complete the following sentences with suitable prepositions of place or time.*

a) . . . . the respondents, few had any experience of working abroad.

b) Industrial production declined gradually . . . . 1976 . . . . 1985.

c) Most workers . . . . the European Union retire before the age . . . . 60.

d) Albert Einstein was born . . . . Germany . . . . 1879.

e) Many flowers open their petals . . . . the morning and close them . . . . night.

f) . . . . the surface, there is no difference . . . . male and female responses.

6. *Complete the following text with suitable prepositions.*

This study sets a). . . . . to answer the

controversial question b) . . . . whether

increased food supply c) . . . . a country

makes a significant contribution d) . . . .

reducing malnutrition e) . . . . children. It uses

data collected f) . . . . seventy-five countries

g) . . . . 1969 and 1987. The findings are that

there was a considerable improvement h) . . . .

the majority i) . . . . countries, despite population

increases j) . . . . the period. However, a clear

distinction was found k) . . . . the poorest

countries (e.g. l) . . . . South Asia), where the

improvement was greatest, and the wealthier states such

as those m) . . . . North Africa. Other factors,

notably the educational level n) . . . . women,

were also found to be critical o) . . . . improving

childhood nutrition.

3.14 Punctuation

1. **Capitals**

   It is difficult to give precise rules about the use of capital letters in modern English. However, they should be used in the following cases:

   a) The first word in a sentence — *In the beginning. . .*

   b) Names of organisations — *Sheffield Hallam University*

   c) Days and months — *Friday 21st July*

   d) Nationality words — *France and the French*

   e) Names of people/places — *Dr Martin Turner from Edinburgh*

   f) Titles (capitalise main words only) — *The Uses of Literacy/ The Duke of Kent*

2. **Apostrophes (')**

   These are one of the most misused features of English punctuation. They are mainly used in two situations:

   a) to show contractions — *It's generally believed . . .*

   NB Contractions are not common in academic English.

   b) with possessives — *The professor's secretary (singular)*

   Students' marks (plural)

3. **Semi-colons (;)**

   They are used to show the link between two connected phrases, when a comma would be too weak and a full stop too strong.

   Twenty people were interviewed for the first study; thirty-three for the second.

   Semi-colons are also used to divide up items in a list when they have a complex structure:

   Among the presents received by the president were three oil paintings of himself, all flattering; a pair of green parrots, which were very noisy; a solid gold medal; and three or four suits of clothes.

   NB Semi-colons are quite rare in most types of writing.

4. **Colons (:)**

   a) to introduce explanations — *The meeting was postponed: the Dean was ill.*

b) to start a list

Two factors were discussed: cultural and social.

c) to introduce a quotation

As Orwell said: 'all art is propaganda'.

cross-reference

2.11 *References and Quotations*

5. **Quotation marks/inverted commas (" "/' ')**

a) Single quotation marks are used to emphasise a word, to give quotations from other writers and to show direct speech:

> The word 'quiz' was first used in the nineteenth century.

> Goodwin's (1977) analysis of habit . . . indicates that, in general, 'it will be more difficult to reverse a trend than to accentuate it'.

> 'Can anyone find the answer?' asked the lecturer.

NB Longer quotations are usually indented (i.e. have a wider margin) or are set in smaller type.

b) Double quotation marks are used to show quotations inside quotations (nested quotations):

> As James remarked: 'Martin's concept of "internal space" requires close analysis.'

c) Quotation marks are used for the names of articles and chapters, but book or journal titles use italics:

> Russell, T. (1995) 'A future for coffee?' *Journal of Applied Marketing* **6** pp.14–17.

6. **Others**

> Hyphens (-) are used with certain words and structures:

> well-engineered/co-operative/3-year-old

> Exclamation marks (!) and question marks (?):

> 'Well!' he shouted, 'Who would believe it?'

> Brackets ( ) are used to contain information of lesser importance:

> There were only thirty-one marriages (out of 13,829) in which 'baker' was listed.

7. *Punctuate the following sentences.*

a) on tuesday june 6 1759 in the church at derby nicolas james married mary dewey

b) professor rowans new book the triumph of capitalism is published in new york

c)   how many people would agree with john lennon when he said all you need is love

d)   the probability was calculated for each of the three faculties physics biology and law

e)   as cammack 1994 points out latin america is creating a new phenomenon democracy without citizens

f)   thousands of new words such as website enter the english language each year

g)   dr tanners latest study focuses on childrens reactions to stress in the playground

h)   she scored 56% on the main course the previous semester she had achieved 67%

8.   *Punctuate the following text.*

the london school of business is offering three new

courses this year economics with psychology introduction

to management and ecommerce the first is taught by

dr jennifer hillary and runs from october to january the

second introduction to management for msc finance

students is offered in the second semester and is

assessed by coursework only professor wangs course in

ecommerce runs in both the autumn and the spring and is

for more experienced students

3.15 Relative Pronouns

cross-reference

2.3   Cohesion

1. **Relative pronouns (*who/whose/where/which/that*) introduce a relative clause.**

    Saturn, *which* is encircled by rings, is much larger than the Earth.

    The college *where* he studied has been closed down.

    The teacher *who* interviewed me was a specialist in ancient music.

    Dr Yamada, *whose* lecture I attended, presented the prizes.

    He wrote about the area *that* I was interested in.

    Which relative pronouns are used for:

    a) places?   b) people?   c) things?   d) possession?

cross-reference

2.5   Definitions

2. *Insert a suitable relative pronoun in these sentences and underline the clause.*

    a) The book . . . . he wanted had been borrowed by someone else.

    b) Beijing, ... she studied for 6 months, used to be called Peking.

    c) Charlie Chaplin, ... was born in England, was a great film comedian.

    d) A hydrometer is an instrument . . . . is used to measure density in liquids.

    e) Few people have heard of the man . . . . invented television.

    f) Mercury, ... is a liquid element, is used in many industrial processes.

3. **As can be seen from the examples above, there are two kinds of relative clauses:**

    a) those which define the subject. In this case the relative clause must be included.

        The college where he studied has been closed down.

    b) those which give additional details. Here the relative clause could be removed and the meaning would still be clear.

        Saturn, which is encircled by rings, is much larger than the Earth.

        In type (b) the relative clause is surrounded by commas (,) brackets ( ) or dashes (–).

    Decide which of the sentences in (2) define the subject.

4. *Decide if the following sentences contain defining (D) or additional detail (A) clauses.*

    a) Akio Morita was the person who invented the Walkman.

    b) The first thing that he did was to introduce a new system of assessment.

    c) The medical school, which has a very good reputation, charges £20,000 per year.

    d) The president (who enjoyed playing jazz) was elected for a second term.

    e) A hurricane is a tropical storm which can do enormous damage.

5. **In defining clauses both** *that* **and** *which* **can be used with things:**

    Toyota is a Japanese company *that/which* makes cars.

    But with clauses that provide additional detail only *which* can be used:

    Volkswagen, *which* is a German company, is a major car producer.

    Add relative clauses to the following sentences to provide additional detail.

    a) The main campus covers 29 hectares and houses six faculties.

    b) The River Nile runs from the mountains of East Africa to the Mediterranean.

    c) Moscow has a population of more than 8 million people.

    d) Nelson Mandela was imprisoned for over 25 years.

    e) Apples are grown in many countries with temperate climates.

6. **In defining clauses where the relative pronoun is the object its use is optional:**

    She applied to the university (*that/which*) her tutor had recommended.

    The course (*that/which*) I wanted to take was not offered this semester.

    The tutor (*who*) she wanted to meet was away for two months.

    When the relative pronoun is the subject it must be included:

    The scientists *who* discovered DNA worked in Cambridge.

Decide if the relative pronouns in the following are necessary. If not, cross them out.

a) It was not known who was responsible for the explosion.

b) The man who I read about was born in Scotland.

c) The book which the professor wrote was remarkably short.

d) Squirrels are mammals that live mainly in trees.

e) The article which she referred to was published last year.

7. *Insert suitable relative pronouns in the gaps below. Write X if the pronoun is optional.*

King Camp Gillette, a). . . . . invention of the

disposable razor blade made his name world-famous,

was an American b) . . . . had spent 40 years

looking for a saleable invention. The idea c) . . . .

. . . . . changed his fortunes occurred in 1895, but he met

considerable difficulties producing a thin, sharp blade

d) . . . . could be made cheaply. He sold

shares in the company to pay for the development work

e) . . . . his partner, William Dickerson, was

doing. In 1903, f). . . . . was their first year of

business, they produced only fifty-one razors. But due

to intensive advertising, g) . . . . potential

Gillette quickly recognised, they rapidly increased sales

to 250,000 two years later. The modern razor, h) . . . .

. . . . is usually double-bladed, is directly related to

the idea i) . . . . Gillette had over a hundred

years ago.

3.16 Singular or Plural?

1. **This can be a confusing area, but the following illustrate the main areas of difficulty:**

   a) Nouns should agree with verbs, and pronouns with nouns.

      Those problems are unique.

      There *are* many *arguments* in favour.

   b) Uncountable nouns and irregular plurals have no final -*s*.

      Most students receive free *tuition*.

      DNA is located in every part; *hair*, nails, *teeth* . . .

   c) General statements normally use the plural.

      State *universities* have lower *fees*.

   d) *Each/every* are followed by singular nouns.

      Every *student* gets financial support.

   e) Two linked nouns should agree.

      Both the *similarities* and *differences* are important.

   Find the mistake in the following and decide what type (a–e above) it is.

   a) The proposal has both advantages and disadvantage.   ( )

   b) A majority of children in Thailand is vaccinated against measles.   ( )

   c) There are few young people in rural area.   ( )

   d) Many places are experiencing an increase in crimes.   ( )

   e) Each towns have their own councils.   ( )

2. **Study the following 'group' phrases.**

singular + plural	plural + plural	plural + uncountable
half the universities	two types of institutions	three areas of enquiry
a range of businesses	various kinds of courses	several fields of research
one of the elements	many species of ants	rates of progress

   Note that if a verb has more than one subject it must be plural, even if the preceding noun is singular:

   Scores of students, some teachers and the president *are* at the meeting.

   Their valuable suggestions and hard work *were* vital.

Certain 'group' nouns, e.g. *team/army/government,* can be followed by either a singular or plural verb:

The team *was* defeated three times last month. (collectively)

The team *were* travelling by train or bus. (separately)

3. *Underline and correct the mistakes in the following extracts from student essays (one per sentence).*

   a) More must be done to solve that problems of development.

   b) The attitude towards this issue vary from person to person.

   c) Many culture from around the world are found in the city.

   d) In the country the people is more friendly.

   e) It is common to move from the countryside to find job.

   f) Huge number of cars use the motorway.

   g) The city have disadvantages such as a high rate of crime.

   h) Public transport lets us move to another places easily.

   i) There are bad pollution due to traffic congestion.

   j) People should not ignore important factors that affect their life.

4. *Read the text and choose the correct alternative.*

A large number of *company/companies has/have* developed *website/websites* in the last few years. Trading using the internet is called *e-commerce/e-commerces,* and *this/these is/are* divided into two main kinds: B2B and B2C. Many *business/businesses* want to use the internet to sell directly to *its/their* customers (B2C), but large numbers have experienced *trouble/troubles* with *security/securities* and other practical issues. In addition, the high start-up costs and the *expense/expenses* of advertising *means/mean* that *this/these company/companies* often struggle to make a profit.

3.17 Time Words and Phrases

cross-reference

| 3.7 | Conjunctions |
| 3.23 | Verbs – Tenses |

1. **Study the use of the following:**

   She went on a training course *for* 6 weeks. (with numbers)

   The report must be finished *by* June 12th. (on or before)

   He has been president *since* 1998. (usually with present perfect)

   They are studying in Bristol *until* March. (end of a period)

   The library was opened 2 years *ago*. (usually with past)

   The hotel is closed *during* the winter. (with noun)

   Before writing he studied over 100 sources. (often followed by *-ing* form; also *after*)

   He applied in May and was accepted two months *later*. (often used with numbers; also *earlier*)

2. **Compare the tenses used with the following phrases:**

   Recently, there has been a sharp rise in internet use. (present perfect)

   Currently, there is a vigorous debate about human rights. (present)

   Last year there was an election in Spain. (past)

   In the last year there has been a sharp rise in inflation. (present perfect)

3. *Study Rachel's schedule for her last business trip and complete the sentences below with a suitable word. It is now April 16th.*

March 12th	Fly London–Milan
March 13th–14th	Conference in Milan
March 15th	Train Milan–Paris
March 16th	Meeting in Paris office
March 17th	Fly Paris–Hong Kong
March 18th–19th	Tour of new development
March 20th	Fly HK–London

   a) . . . . month Rachel made a business trip.

   b) . . . . her trip she visited three countries.

   c) . . . . March 18th she had travelled 11,000 kilometres.

   d) She was away from home . . . . nine days altogether.

   e) A month . . . . she was in Paris.

   f) She stayed in Hong Kong . . . . March 20th.

   g) . . . . she is writing a report on her trip.

4. *Choose the best alternative in each case.*

a) *Currently/recently* she has been researching the life cycle of a species of wasp.

b) She lived in France *until/during* the war broke out, and then she went home.

c) Professor Yung has worked here *since/for* sixteen years.

d) *Last month/in the last month* a new book was published on the subject.

e) Applications must be received *by/on* November 25th.

f) *Since/during* her arrival last May she has reorganised the department.

g) *During/for* the winter most farmers in the region find work in the towns.

5. *Complete the following text with a suitable word or phrase.*

EATING OUT

a) . . . . the last few decades there has been a significant change in eating habits in the UK. b) . . . . the early 1980s eating out in restaurants and cafes has increased steadily. There are several reasons for this trend.

50 years c) . . . . most women were housewives, and cooked for their families every day. But d) . . . ., with more women working outside the home, less time has been available for food preparation. e) . . . ., 71% of women aged 20–45 are at work, and f) . . . . 2015 it is estimated that this will rise to 84%.

Another factor is the growth in disposable income, which has risen significantly g) . . . . the late 1970s. With more money in their pockets people are more likely to save the trouble of shopping and cooking by visiting their local restaurant.

6.   *Study the details of Napoleon's life, and complete the biography below.*

1769	born in Corsica
1784	entered military school in Paris
1789	French revolution started
1793	promoted to brigadier general
1796	appointed to command army of Italy; married Josephine
1799	returned from Egypt and became First Consul of France
1807	France controlled most of continental Europe
1810	divorced Josephine and married Marie-Louise, daughter of Austrian emperor
1812	forced to retreat from Russia
1814	exiled to island of Elba
1815	defeated at battle of Waterloo and exiled to island of St Helena
1821	died in exile

Napoleon entered military school at the age of 15, 5 years a) . . . . the start of the French revolution. He rose quickly, becoming brigadier general at 24 and commander of the Italian army three years b) . . . . At 30 he was effectively the French dictator, and due to his military genius France controlled most of Europe c) . . . . 1807. When he divorced his first wife, Josephine, in 1810, they had been married d) . . . . 14 years. His campaigns were successful e) . . . . 1812, but in that year the disastrous retreat from Moscow marked the start of his decline. However, f) . . . . his years of absolute power he had made significant changes to European law and government. Although he died nearly 200 years g) . . . ., Napoleon's influence is still felt throughout the European continent.

3.18 Verbs – Formality

cross-reference

3.2   *Academic Vocabulary*

1. **A feature of most academic writing is a tendency to use rather formal verbs to express the writer's meaning accurately:**

    . . . supply of energy required to *accelerate* the growth . . .

    . . . the development that is *envisaged* here needs to be not only sustainable . . .

    In spoken English we would be more likely to use *speed up* and *imagined.*

    Study the list below and find a synonym in each case.

    NB Some of these verbs, e.g. *hold*, are used in academic writing with a special meaning.

Verb	Example of use
to adapt	the health system has been *adapted* from France
to arise	a similar situation *arises* when we look at younger children
to carry out	the largest study was *carried out* in Finland
to characterise	developing countries are *characterised* by . . . .
to clarify	the project was designed to *clarify* these contradictions
to concentrate on	that study *concentrated on* older children
to be concerned with	the programme is *concerned* primarily *with* . . .
to demonstrate	further research has *demonstrated* that few factors . . .
to determine	the water content was experimentally *determined*
to discriminate	a failure to *discriminate* between the two species
to emphasise	the 1987 report *emphasised* energy efficiency
to establish	the northern boundary was *established* first
to exhibit	half of the patients *exhibited* signs of improvement
to focus on	her work *focused on* female managers
to generate	a question which has *generated* a range of responses
to hold	Newton's second Law, $F=ma$, *holds* everywhere
to identify	three main areas have been *identified*
to imply	previous research *implies* that size is a good predictor
to indicate	all the surveys *indicate* that employees prefer pay rises
to interact	understand how the two systems *interact*
to interpret	the conclusion can be *interpreted* as a limited success
to manifest	as *manifested* in anti-social behaviour

to overcome	both difficulties were *overcome* in the first week
to predict	the study *predicts* that productivity will decline next year
to propose	they *propose* that social class is the main factor
to prove	the use of solar power is *proving* successful
to recognise	he is now *recognised* as a leading expert
to relate to	the pattern was *related to* both social and physical factors
to supplement	the diet was *supplemented* with calcium and iodine
to undergo	the system *underwent* major changes in the 1980s
to yield	both surveys *yielded* mixed results

2. **Select the better alternative in each case.**

a) The survey *proved/yielded* a surprising amount of information on student politics.

b) This question *arose/manifested* when older students were examined.

c) Both writers attempt to *demonstrate/imply* that older employees are more reliable.

d) Darwin *held/indicated* very strong views on this issue.

e) It must be *proved/emphasised* that these results are only provisional.

f) One of the chimpanzees *supplemented/exhibited* signs of nervousness.

g) Freud was *concerned/identified* primarily with middle class patients.

h) The study was *generated/carried out* to explore the issue of religious tolerance.

3. **Insert a suitable verb from the box below into each gap.**

| overcome | predict | demonstrate | interpret |
| discriminate | recognise | clarify | focus on |

a) The results clearly . . . . that younger children learn quicker.

b) This paper attempts to . . . . the confusion surrounding studies of infertility.

c) Social class must be . . . . as a leading factor in educational success.

d) His study fails to . . . . between the various types of reinforced concrete.

e) It seems profitable to . . . . the record of smaller companies.

f) The noises made by whales have been . . . . in several ways.

g) This problem was . . . . by reversing the direction of the gas flow.

h) Most experts failed to . . . . the collapse of Soviet power in 1989.

3.19 Verbs – Modal

cross-reference

3.5   Caution

1. **Modal verbs used in academic writing tend to have three main meanings:**

    a) Ability

    May and *can* are similar but *can* is more common:

    The assessment . . . *may* be made in a variety of ways

    . . . with smaller samples this method *cannot* be used . . .

    . . . one faculty *can* have more than one academic programme . . .

    b) Degrees of certainty

    Will and *should* are used for predictions of near certainty (*will* is stronger):

    . . . in the knowledge that the parent *will* be there when needed.

    Improved facilities *should* lead to lower staff turnover.

    May and *might* both suggest possibility:

    Landfill carbon sequestration *might* supplement fossil fuel combustion . . .

    . . . multiple factors *may* lead to a psychiatric consultation . . .

    Would and *could* are used in conditional situations (not always with *if*):

    . . . or *would* we conclude that the observation is uninformative?

    . . . estimates of the model's parameters *could* conceivably be computed . . .

    c) Degrees of obligation

    Must suggests strong obligation, *should* is for recommendations:

    To obtain a total estimate . . . several approximations *must* be used

    A primary research emphasis . . . *should* then be on identifying . . .

2. *Complete the following sentences with a suitable modal of ability.*

    a) The question is whether democracy . . . . survive in such difficult conditions.

    b) Fifty years ago a new house . . . . be bought for £1,500.

c) Students . . . . be expected to write more than one long essay a week.

d) The mistakes of past historians . . . . now be clearly seen.

e) Jenkins (1976) argued that aluminium . . . . be used in place of steel.

3. *Complete the following with a suitable modal of certainty.*

   a) It . . . . not be surprising if the company were bought by a rival.

   b) Various social situations . . . . lead to a child's loss of confidence.

   c) Other studies confirm that a permanent shift in transport use . . . . occur.

   d) By 2020 most children . . . . have internet access by the age of 5.

   e) If the pressure is lowered, the reaction . . . . take place more quickly.

   f) In the long term, solar power . . . . make a significant contribution.

   g) Many seventeenth-century farmers . . . . write their names.

4. *Use a suitable modal of obligation to complete the following.*

   a) Students studying abroad . . . . take some of their favourite music with them.

   b) All books . . . . be returned to the main library by June 19th.

   c) First-year undergraduates . . . . take at least three modules from the list below.

   d) The second part of the essay . . . . focus on the differences in the results.

5. *In the following sentences, the meaning changes according to the modal verb used. Find two possibilities, giving the meanings in each case.*

   Example:

   Using the internet means the company *can* sell its products worldwide. (ability)

   Using the internet means the company *might* sell its products worldwide. (possibility)

   a) The poorest people . . . . be helped by improving the supply of water.   (   )

The poorest people . . . . be helped
by improving the supply of water.   (   )

b) Tribal leaders of the first century BC . . . .
    have used writing.   (   )

    Tribal leaders of the first century BC . . . .
    have used writing.   (   )

c) Few people . . . . agree to take part in the
    experiment.   (   )

    Few people . . . . agree to take part in the
    experiment.   (   )

d) Care . . . . always be taken when
    interpreting nineteenth-century data.   (   )

    Care . . . . always be taken when
    interpreting nineteenth-century data.   (   )

e) By the mid-twenty-first century poverty . . . . be
    abolished.   (   )

    By the mid-twenty-first century poverty . . . . be
    abolished.   (   )

f) Repeating the study . . . . confirm their
    findings.   (   )

    Repeating the study . . . . confirm their
    findings.   (   )

3.20 Verbs – Passives

cross-reference

2.13   *Style*

1. **The passive is used when the writer wants to focus on the result, not on the cause:**

   The book was written by my father. (passive)

   My father wrote the book. (active)

   In the first sentence, the emphasis is on the book, in the second on the writer. So the passive is often used in written English when the cause (a person or thing) is less important or unknown.

   The treaty *will be signed* next year. (by someone)

   The tower *was destroyed* a century ago. (by something)

   The cause of the action can be shown by adding *by* . . .:

   The ship was launched in 1908 *by Princess Mary*.

2. **The passive is also used in written work to provide a more impersonal style:**

   The findings *were evaluated*.

   Change the following into the passive.

   a)   We collected the data and compared the two groups.

   b)   I interviewed 120 people in three social classes.

   c)   They checked the results and found several errors.

   d)   We will make an analysis of the findings.

cross-reference

3.3   *Adverbs*

3. **An adverb is often inserted in a passive form to add detail:**

   This process is *commonly* called 'networking'.

   Change the following sentences from active to passive and insert a suitable adverb from the box below.

   Example:

   A storm damaged 40% of the houses in the port.

   40% of the houses in the port were badly damaged by a storm.

   a)   The Connors family ran the company until 1981.

   b)   They had built the house near the station.

   c)   Picasso painted the portrait of the old man.

   d)   They provided pencils for all students in the exam.

   e)   Doctors tested over 550 people for the disease over a 3-year period.

   f)   The researchers calculated the percentages to three decimal places.

g) They called their business the Universal Trading Company.

conveniently	optimistically	helpfully	brilliantly
regularly	precisely	profitably	badly

4. **In most texts the active and the passive are mixed.**

Read the following article and underline the passives.

BOOTS THE CHEMISTS

When John Boot died at 45, he was worn out by the strain of establishing his herbal medicine business. He had worked his way up from his early years as a farm labourer to be the owner of a substantial business. He was born in 1815, became a member of a Methodist chapel in Nottingham, and later moved to the city. Concerned by the situation of the poor, who were unable to afford a doctor, in 1849 he opened a herbal medicine shop which was called the British and American Botanic Establishment. In the early stages John was helped financially by his father in law, while his mother provided herbal knowledge.

On his death in 1860 the business was taken over by his wife, and she was soon assisted by their 10-year-old son, Jesse. He quickly showed the business ability which transformed his father's shop into a national business. He opened more shops in poor districts of the city and pioneered advertising methods. Another innovation was to do all his business in cash, rather than offering credit.

5. *Could all the passives in the text above be replaced by the active?*
    What would be the result if most of them were?

6. **The passive is used more in written than in spoken English, but should not be overused, as it can give a very formal tone. In the following text, which continues the history of Boots, passives are used throughout.** *Change some of them into the active.*

In 1889 he was introduced to Florence Rowe, the daughter of a bookseller, while on holiday. Her influence was felt by the business after they were married: the product range was enlarged to include stationery and books. In addition she was responsible for the introduction of the Boots subscription library and in-store cafes.

During World War I the factories were used to make a variety of products from sterilisers to gas masks. But by 1920 Jesse was being attacked by arthritis and was worried by the economic prospects. Boots was sold to an American rival for £2m. This, however, was made bankrupt during the Depression and Boots was then bought by a British group for £6m, while Jesse's son, John, was made chairman. The famous No. 7 cosmetics range was launched in the 1930s. In the 1939–45 war the saccharin equivalent to 700,000 tons of sugar was produced in the factories.

3.21 Verbs and Prepositions

1. **The following verbs are generally used with these prepositions:**

Verb + prep.	Example
add to	The bad weather *added to* the general's difficulties.
agree with	Yu (1977) *agrees with* Martin and Jenks (1989).
associate with	Monetarism is an economic policy *associated with* Mrs Thatcher.
believe in	The survey showed that 65% *believed in* life after death.
blame for	He *blamed* unfair questions *for* his poor exam results.
concentrate on (*also: focus on*)	She dropped all her hobbies to *concentrate on* her work.
consist of	Parliament *consists of* two Houses: the Commons and the Lords.
depend on (*also: rely on*)	The company *depends on* IT for a rapid flow of sales data.
derive from	All modern computers *derive from* wartime decoding machines.
divide into	Trees are *divided into* two main types: conifers and deciduous.
invest in	Far more money needs to be *invested in* primary education.
learn from	All successful students *learn from* their mistakes.
pay for	Goods delivered in April must be *paid for* by June 30th.
point out	Goodson (2001) *points out* the dangers of overspecialisation.
specialise in	This department *specialises in* French-Canadian poetry.

2. *Complete the following with suitable verbs and prepositions.*

   a) The enquiry . . . . the cause of the accident, not the consequences.

   b) Dr Cracknell . . . . that there were only two weeks before the deadline.

   c) Fewer British students are . . . . foreign languages.

   d) The theory of relativity will always be . . . . Albert Einstein.

   e) A football pitch is . . . . two halves.

   f) A series of strikes were . . . . the decline in production during May.

g) Millions of men died for the cause they . . . .
. . . .

h) Every nation needs a public transport system it can . . . .
. . . .

3. **With certain verbs more than one preposition is possible (note the change of meaning in some cases).**

Verb + preposition	Example
compare to/with	The stock market has been *compared with/to* a casino.
look at/into	The evidence needs to be *looked at/into* more carefully.
look for	Most students use search engines to *look for* information.
apply to	He *applied to* the committee for a grant.
apply for	To *apply for* the job three forms must be completed.

4. *Choose suitable verbs and prepositions from (1) and (3) to complete the following text.*

The new model of camera, the Alpha 616, a) . . . .
. . . . the previous model, the Alpha 615. The
new model b) . . . . a standard camera
with a small tape recorder c) . . . . it.
This allows the photographer to talk to the camera. The
marketing unit d) . . . . the camera
market carefully and discovered that many people forget
where they take pictures. These people can now e) . . . . .
. . . . the Alpha 616 to remember for them.

The Alpha company has f) . . . . over
£2 million . . . . the new product. g) . . . .
. . . . other projects this may seem a small amount,
but it is not a large firm. It is hoped that customers will
h) . . . . over £100 . . . . the
camera, which the company will i) . . . .
for significant profits next year.

3.22 Verbs of Reference

1. **Referring verbs are used to summarise another writer's ideas.**

    Wilsher *argued* that the single play had been consigned to television history.

    Heffernan (1972) *found* that adaptation to prison was facilitated by . . .

    They may also be used to introduce a quotation.

    . . . as Peter Huber has *observed*, 'Coal itself is yesterday's landfill . . .'

2. **Most of these verbs are followed by a noun clause beginning with *that*.**

    a) The following mean that the writer is presenting a case:

argue	claim	consider	hypothesise
suggest	believe	think	state

    Martins (1975) *claimed* that many mergers led to lower profits.

    b) A second group describe a reaction to another writer's position:

accept	admit	agree	deny	doubt

    Handlesmith *doubts* Martins's claim that lower profits resulted from . . .

    c) Others include:

assume	conclude	discover	explain	imply
indicate	maintain	presume	reveal	show

    Patel (2003) *assumes* that inflation will remain low.

    Borovna *implies* a close relation between the Queen and her minister.

3. *Write a sentence referring to what the following writers said (more than one verb may be suitable). Use the past tense.*

    Example: Z: 'My research shows that cats are cleverer than dogs'.

    Z claimed/argued that cats were cleverer than dogs.

    a) A: 'You could be right. I may have made a mistake in my estimate.'

    b) B: 'I did not say that sheep were faster than horses.'

    c) C: 'Whales are very intelligent animals.'

    d) D: 'I support A's position on cats and dogs.'

    e) E: 'I'm not sure, but cows probably get cold in winter.'

f) F: 'After much research, I've found that pigs can't fly.'

g) G: 'On my travels in the jungle I found a new type of frog.'

h) H: 'I think it unlikely that cats can learn to talk.'

i) I: 'Somebody should compare mouse behaviour with rat behaviour.'

j) J: 'There may be a link between health and the seasons.'

4. **A small group of verbs is followed by (somebody/thing +** *for* **+ noun/gerund):**

> blame   censure   commend   condemn   criticise
>
> Lee (1998) *blamed* foreign investors for the panic.
>
> NB All except *commend* have a negative meaning.

A final group is followed by (somebody/thing + *as* + noun/gerund):

> assess   characterise   classify   define   describe
>
> evaluate   identify   interpret   portray   present
>
> Terry *interprets* rising oil prices as a result of Asian recovery.

5. *Rewrite the following statements using verbs from the lists in (4).*

> Example: K: 'X's work is responsible for many of our current economic problems.'
>
> K blamed X's work for many of our current economic problems.

a) L: 'She was very careless about her research methods.'

b) M: 'There are three main species of bees.'

c) N: 'The cat family are the kings of the animal world.'

d) O: 'I'm sure that dogs bark because they are nervous.'

e) P: 'Trying to estimate the number of animal species is like shooting in the dark.'

f) Q: 'Darwin was the greatest naturalist of the nineteenth century.'

g) R: 'An insect is a six-legged arthropod.'

h) S: 'Queen Victoria was a short, rather fat woman with dark eyes.'

i) T: 'Gregor Mendel can be considered the founder of modern genetics.'

3.23 Verbs – Tenses

1. *Decide which tenses are used in the following examples (verbs in italics) and complete the table to explain why.*

   a) According to Hoffman (1996), small firms *respond* more rapidly to changes . . .

   b) Currently, inflation in the US *is rising* while imports *are falling*.

   c) Since November there *has been* a significant increase in cases of influenza.

   d) In the last three years more students *have been working* part-time.

   e) After the war there *was* a sharp rise in divorce.

   f) During 1998 they *were developing* a new system.

   g) The study was published in June. It showed that in 1998 and 1999 profits *had increased* by 55%.

   h) The forecast concludes that interest rates *will reach* 7.5% next year.

	Tense	Reason for use
a		
b		
c		
d		
e		
f		
g		
h		

   NB In the last month/year/decade = present perfect (unfinished period).

   Last month/year/decade = simple past (finished period).

2. *Complete the following sentences by selecting the most suitable tenses.*

   a) Home ownership . . . . (rise) steadily since 1950.

b) GM . . . . (stand for) genetically modified.

c) Last year the police . . . . (record) a record number of crimes.

d) When she died in 1986 she . . . . (write) over fifty books.

e) By 2050 average temperatures . . . . (be) at least 2 degrees higher.

f) At the moment the bank . . . . (consider) a merger proposal from Barclays.

g) When the market crashed the company . . . . (build) three hotels in Asia.

h) Lee (1965) . . . . (dispute) Sakamoto's theory.

i) In the last 6 years inflation . . . . (fall) sharply in Europe.

3. Simple or continuous?

a) In general, the continuous is used to focus on the activity itself or to stress its temporary nature. Compare the following:

She has been writing that report for 6 days.   (activity)

He is writing a travel article.   (temporarily)

She writes children's books. (usually)

b) Also note that certain verbs are rarely used in the continuous. They are state verbs like *prefer*, *own* and *believe*. Another similar group is known as performative verbs (*assume, deny, promise, refuse, suggest*).

4. *Select either simple or continuous in each case:*

a) The team at Cambridge . . . . (work) on a rare type of brain disease.

b) He . . . . (believe) he will finish the study early next year.

c) This magazine . . . . (look for) a writer on new technology.

d) In the late 1990s she was working on rice plants but now she . . . . (research) potatoes.

e) The average age of marriage in Britain . . . . (rise) by 6 years since 1970.

f) The company . . . . (own) factories in twelve countries.

g) Most people in the city . . . . (live) within two kilometres of their work.

h) Dr McPherson . . . . (attend) a conference in South America this week.

cross-reference

3.17   *Time Words and Phrases*
3.20   *Verbs – Passives*

5. **When writing paragraphs, it is important to be clear about which time phrases control the tenses of verbs:**

> For years, the condition of the family *has produced* some of the strongest debate heard in America. The statistics of collapse *have appeared* simple and clear. The proportion of children born outside marriage *rose* from 18% in 1980 to 33% in 1999. The share of households made up of two parents and their children *fell* from 45% in 1960 to only 23% in 2000.

In this case, the time phrase *For years* controls the tense of the first two sentences (present perfect). The following two sentences are in the simple past because of the dates *1980, 1999, 1960* and *2000* which show finished periods.

6. *Read the text below and select the most suitable tense for each verb in brackets, considering the time phrases in italics.*

> *For a long time* gardeners a) . . . . (suspect) that using green fingers is just as effective as talking softly to plants to encourage growth. Scientists b) . . . . (develop) a robot that strokes young plants to make them grow stronger and faster. But after research *a year ago* c) . . . . (confirm) that plants need the human touch, scientists at Greenwich University d) . . . . (develop) the stroking machine they call Dr Green.

> Dr Green e) . . . . (be display) *at the last Chelsea Flower Show*, where it f) . . . . (demonstrate) the technique of brushing the tips of young plants to produce stronger specimens. David Carey, who is leading the research, g) . . . . (say) that the machine could avoid the use of chemicals.

> *Currently*, Dr Green h) . . . . (be test) on a large scale by a commercial grower. Stroking plants once a day i) . . . . (make) them 30% stronger, which is what you need before you plant them out. *When another kind of plant was stroked* once a week, it j) . . . . (develop) increased insect resistance. The research team hope that a cheap version of Dr Green k) . . . . (be available) to amateur gardeners *by 2007*.

4. Writing Models

Student Introduction

There are various possible formats for different types of essays, as well as non-academic texts such as letters and CVs. For instance, if a selection of formal letters is studied it will be seen that different styles of headings and layout are used by different organisations. However, the following models are provided so that students can use the outlines confident that they will be acceptable in most situations.

Many courses require students to conduct a survey, so unit 4.3 *Reporting and Designing Surveys* provides a model for a survey report. Unit 4.4 *Taking Ideas from Sources* gives a model for the vital process of note-making, paraphrasing and referencing. Comparison and discussion are common components of essay titles, and the models given here show one way of answering the questions. However, it must be remembered that both comparison and discussion (plus other elements) may be needed in the same essay.

Faculties and departments may give new students guidance (e.g. handbooks) about what is required in terms of style and layout, and if this is not available it is worth asking your teacher whether it is acceptable to use sub-headings, numbering and other layout features.

4.1 Formal Letters

cross-reference

3.1 Abbreviations

1. **You have applied for a place on an MA course at a British university. This is the letter you have received in reply.**

---

a)   **Arts & Social Sciences Admissions Office**
Wye House
Central Campus
University of Borchester
Borchester BR3 5HT
United Kingdom

b)   Ms P Tan
54 Sydney Road
Rowborough RB1 6FD

c)   Ref: MB/373

d)   3 May 2006

e)   Dear Ms Tan

f)   **Application for MA International Studies**

g)   Further to your recent application, I would like to invite you to the university for an informal interview on Tuesday 21st May at 11 am. You will be able to meet the course supervisor, Dr Schmidt, and look round the department.

h)   A map of the campus and instructions for finding the university are enclosed.

i)   Please let me know if you will be able to attend on the date given.

j)   Yours sincerely

k)   *M. Bramble*

l)   Mick Bramble
Administrative Assistant
Arts & Social Sciences

Enc.

Label the following features of formal letters with the letters (a–l) from the left margin above.

(*d*) Date	(. . .) Ending
(. . .) Request for response	(. . .) Greetings
(. . .) Address of recipient	(. . .) Address of sender
(. . .) Further details	(. . .) Reason for writing
(. . .) Sender's reference	(. . .) Subject headline
(. . .) Signature	(. . .) Writer's name and title

Note the following points.

a) When writing to somebody whose name you do not know, e.g. The Manager, use *Dear Sir* and *Yours faithfully*.

b) A formal letter generally uses the family name in the greeting (*Dear Ms Tan*). Certain organisations may, however, use a first name with a family name or even a first name alone (*Dear Jane Tan/Dear Jane*).

c) If the sender includes a reference it is helpful to quote it in your reply.

2. *Write a reply to Mr Bramble making the following points:*

a) You will attend the interview on the date given.

b) You would like to have the interview one hour later, because of train times.

> 54 Sydney Road
> Rowborough RB1 6FD

3. *Study the following newspaper advert. You have decided to apply for this job. Make notes for your letter of application, then write the letter, paying attention to layout as well as content.*

cross-reference

4.2 CVs

STAFF REQUIRED FOR RECEPTION WORK AT CITY HOTEL

We are looking for enthusiastic and helpful receptionists (m/f) to join our team. Candidates should be well-presented and able to speak at least two languages. Hotel experience not necessary as training will be given. Ability to get on with people and work in a team more important. Some evening and weekend work. Good conditions and rates of pay.

Apply in writing with CV and covering letter to: The Manager, Hotel Nelson, Queens Road, Rowborough RB2 4RN quoting Ref. EN2.

4.2 CVs

1. CV stands for *curriculum vitae* (also known as a *résumé*). A CV is a summary of your education and work experience, often requested by prospective employers. Most professionals store their CVs electronically so that they can be updated when necessary.

2. There is considerable debate about the format of CVs, and much depends on your experience and the area you are working in. The example given below is relatively short, as would be expected for a recent graduate.

Sarah Ann Atkins
DOB 19.6.80
Email: saatkins@virgin.net

Career aim

To develop my experience in marketing in a senior managerial role, using my knowledge of European languages.

Career history

2004–present	**Marketing Assistant, Eastern Foods, Derby**
	In my current post I am part of a team involved in marketing our products throughout the UK. I have helped organise several campaigns and given presentations in connection with these.
2000–1	**English Teacher, Montpellier, France**
	During my year abroad I taught English at a school in Montpellier, which not only helped strengthen my French but also gave me valuable lessons in self-reliance.

Academic qualifications

2004	**MBA** (Rowborough University Business School)
2003	**BA** (Hons) 2:1 in European Languages (University of Leeds) with distinction in spoken French

Skills

Languages:	knowledge of Spanish and French (advanced)/Italian (good)
ICT:	competence with the following applications: Word, Excel, Powerpoint
Personal	I would describe myself as outgoing, friendly and a good communicator. I apply these qualities to establishing good customer relations and working with colleagues as part of a team.

NB

a)   The above format is only one possibility and it is worth looking at other CVs to compare layouts.

b)   Your address and phone number should be in your covering letter, not on the CV.

c)   List qualifications and experience in reverse chronological order, starting with the most recent. Prospective employers are mainly interested in your latest achievements.

d)   Do not clutter the CV with details of hobbies which are irrelevant to the job you are applying for. Similarly, your early education is unimportant.

e)   Do not just give job titles but explain in detail what you did.

f)   Only give references if asked to do so.

3.   *Prepare a CV for yourself. First make notes of all the important information (with dates), using similar headings to those in the example above. Then organise it as clearly as possible. Finally, type it on a computer and store it so it can be updated in future.*

4.3 Reporting and Designing Surveys

1. Surveys, in which people are asked questions about their opinions or behaviour, are a common feature of academic work, especially in fields such as education, psychology and social sciences.

   What are the reasons for carrying out surveys? List your ideas below.

   a)

   b)

   c)

2. *Study the report of a survey carried out on a university campus. Complete the report by inserting suitable words from the box below into the gaps.*

sample	conducted	slightly	respondents
random	questions	majority	questioned
mentioned	interviewees	common	questionnaire
generally	minority		

   ### STUDENT EXPERIENCE OF PART-TIME WORK

   Introduction

   With the introduction of course fees and the related increase in student debt, more students are finding it necessary to work part-time. The survey was a) . . . . to find out how this work affects student life and study. The research was done by asking students selected at b) . . . . on the campus to complete a c) . . . . (see Appendix 1). Fifty students were d) . . . . on Saturday April 23rd, with approximately equal numbers of male and female students.

   Findings

   Of the e) . . . ., 30% currently had part-time jobs, 20% had had part-time jobs, but half had never done any work during university semesters (see Table 1). f) . . . . who were working or who had worked were next asked about the reasons for taking the jobs. The most common reason was lack of money (56%), but many students said that they found the work useful experience (32%) and others g) . . . . social benefits (12%).

Table 1. Do you have or have you had a part-time job?

	Men	Women	Total	%
Have job now	8	7	15	30
Had job before	4	6	10	20
Never had job	14	11	25	50

The twenty-five students with work experience were next asked about the effects of the work on their studies. A significant h) . . . . (64%) claimed that there were no negative effects at all. However, 24% said that their academic work suffered i) . . . ., while a small j) . . . . (12%) reported serious adverse results, such as tiredness in lectures and falling marks.

Further k) . . . . examined the nature of the work that the students did. The variety of jobs was surprising, from van driver to busker, but the most l) . . . . areas were catering and bar work (44%) and secretarial (32%). Most students worked between 10 and 15 hours per week, though two (8%) worked over 25 hours. Rates of pay were m) . . . . near the national minimum wage, and averaged £5.20 per hour.

The final question invited students to comment on their experience of part-time work. Many (44%) made the point that students should be given larger grants so that they could concentrate on their studies full-time, but others felt that they gained something from the experience, such as meeting new people and getting insights into various work environments. One student said that she had met her current boyfriend while working in a city centre restaurant.

Conclusions

It is clear that part-time work is now a common aspect of student life. Many students find jobs at some point in their studies, but an overwhelming majority (88%) of those deny that it has a damaging effect on their studies. Most students work for only 2–3 hours per day on average, and a significant number claim some positive results from their employment.

Obviously, our survey was limited to a relatively small n) . . . . by time constraints, and a fuller study might modify our findings in various ways.

3. *Question 1 is given above Table 1. What were the other questions in this survey?*

Using the report above, write possible questions 2–7.

2.

3.

4.

5.

6.

7.

4. *What is the main tense in (a)* **Introduction** *and* **Findings,** *(b)* **Conclusion***?*

    Explain the reason for the difference.

5. **Questionnaire design.**
    Which is the better question?

    i)   How old are you?

    ii)   Are you (a) under 20, (b) between 21 and 30, (c) over 30?

6. *What is the main difference between the two questions?*

    i)   What do you think of university students?

    ii)   Do you think university students are (a) lazy, (b) hardworking, (c) average?

7. *How many questions should your questionnaire contain?*

    When designing your questionnaire:

    a)   Limit the number of questions so the respondent can answer them in a minute or two. Long and complicated questionnaires will not receive accurate replies.

    b)   Questions should be clear and simple, and not be too personal.

    c)   Closed questions (6ii) are easier to process, but open questions (6i) will collect a wider range of responses.

    d)   You should try asking the questions to a classmate before beginning the full survey, and be ready to modify any that were not clear.

8. *You are preparing a survey on one of the following subjects. Write a questionnaire of no more than six questions to collect the most useful data.*

    a)   How overseas students learn vocabulary

    b)   Student attitudes to the cinema

    c)   A comparison of undergraduate and post-graduate leisure activities

4.4 Taking Ideas from Sources

cross-reference

1.6 *Selecting Key Points*

1. **You have been told to write an essay on the following title:**

   Can money buy happiness?

   You have found the following text which seems relevant to this topic. It is part of an article by A. Penec in a journal called *Applied Econometrics* (volume 44, pages 18–27) published in 2003.

   Read it, and underline the key points.

   THE MEASUREMENT OF HAPPINESS

   In the last 50 years there has been no apparent increase in personal happiness in Western nations, despite steadily growing economies. In both Europe and the USA surveys have found no greater level of happiness since the 1950s, which seems strange since wealthier people generally claim to be happier than poorer people. In America, for example, more than a third of the richest group said they were 'very happy', while only half this number of the poorest made the same claim. Although it would be logical to expect that rising national wealth would lead to greater national happiness, this has not happened. Individually, more money does seem to increase happiness, but when everyone gets richer, no-one appears to feel better.

   Economists have recently paid more attention to studying happiness, instead of the more traditional GDP per person. One suggestion has been that people rapidly get used to improvements, and therefore devalue them. Central heating is a good example: whereas 30 years ago it was a luxury item, today it is standard in nearly every home.

2. **The text contains four key points:**

   a) In the last 50 years there has been no apparent increase in personal happiness in Western nations, despite steadily growing economies.

   b) . . . which seems strange since wealthier people generally claim to be happier than poorer people.

   c) Individually, more money does seem to increase happiness, but when everyone gets richer, no-one appears to feel better.

   d) One suggestion has been that people rapidly get used to improvements, and therefore devalue them.

cross-reference

1.7   *Note-making*
1.8   *Paraphrasing*

3. **The next step is to make notes of these points, using paraphrase:**

    a) Although W. economies expanded since 1950s, no parallel growth in happiness.

    b) But most rich people say they are happier than poor.

    c) Money appears to make individuals happier but not society as a whole.

    d) People soon get accustomed to developments, so don't appreciate them.

cross-reference

2.11   *References and
        Quotations*

4. **These points can now be combined into one paragraph of your essay, using conjunctions where necessary, and including a reference to your source:**

    Penec (2003) argues that although Western economies have expanded since the 1950s, there has been no parallel growth in happiness. Surveys indicate that rich people generally say they are happier than poor people, but it appears that although individuals may become happier society as a whole does not. One possible answer is that people soon become accustomed to improvements and so do not appreciate them.

5. *Continue the same process with the next section of the text to produce another paragraph of your essay:*

    A further explanation for the failure of wealth to increase happiness is the tendency for people to compare their own position to that of their neighbours. Studies show that people would prefer to have a lower income, if their colleagues got less, rather than a higher income while colleagues got more. In other words, happiness seems to depend on feeling better off than other people, rather than on any absolute measure of wealth. Further research suggests that having free time is also closely linked to happiness, so that the pattern of working harder in order to buy more goods is unlikely to increase well-being. Yet Western societies generally encourage employees to spend as much time at work as possible.

6. **Notes on the second section might be:**

    a) Happiness often depends on feeling wealthier than others.

    b) People believe that leisure = happiness, so working longer to get extra goods won't lead to happiness.

    These points could summarised as:

    Another explanation Penec presents is that happiness is often dependent on a comparison with others, so that if neighbours are also getting richer there is no apparent improvement. A further factor relates to leisure, which is widely equated with happiness. Consequently the idea of increasing workload to be able to purchase more goods or services is not going to result in greater happiness.

7. **The entire section of your essay which makes use of this source is as follows:**

Penec (2003) argues that although Western economies have expanded since the 1950s, there has been no parallel growth in happiness. Surveys indicate that rich people generally say they are happier than poor people, but it appears that although individuals may become happier society as a whole does not. One possible answer is that people soon become accustomed to improvements and so do not appreciate them.

Another explanation Penec presents is that happiness is often dependent on a comparison with others, so that if neighbours are also getting richer there is no apparent improvement. A further factor relates to leisure, which is widely equated with happiness. Consequently the idea of increasing workload to be able to purchase more goods or services is not going to result in greater happiness.

The reference section at the end of the essay should include the following:

Penec, A. (2003) 'The measurement of happiness' *Applied Econometrics* **44** p.18

4.5　Comparison Essay

Read the essay carefully and find:

a)　a definition

b)　an example

c)　a generalisation

d)　a phrase expressing cause and effect

e)　a passive

f)　a phrase expressing caution

g)　three synonyms for *internet-based teaching*

COMPARE CLASSROOM LEARNING WITH INTERNET-BASED TEACHING. IS THE LATTER LIKELY TO REPLACE THE FORMER?

Since the late 1990s internet-based teaching (also known as e-education) has emerged as a potential rival to traditional classroom learning. It normally involves having access to a secure site on the internet where a graded series of lessons are available, and which have assignments sent and returned by email. Although on-line courses are now offered by many institutions, it is by no means clear that they offer real advantages compared to classroom education. Little research has been done so far on their effectiveness, but this essay sets out to examine the arguments on both sides and attempts to draw conclusions from them.

Two main advantages of internet use in education are put forward. Firstly, it is seen as more economical, in that once a course is prepared, it can be used by large numbers of students. The savings made by not having to employ so many teachers should be reflected in cheaper course fees. The second benefit is convenience; instead of having to attend classes at fixed times and places, students are free to study when they choose and progress at their own pace. Furthermore, by studying from home there is no need to travel to the college or university, saving both time and money. A student living in a small town in China, for example, can now study a course at an American college without the worry of travelling, accommodation or homesickness.

Despite the considerations mentioned above, classroom learning shows no signs of being replaced by e-learning. It seems that face-to-face contact with a teacher is still widely regarded as the best way for students to make progress, despite the expense and inconvenience involved. Not only the personal contact with a teacher, but also the support and encouragement gained from being part of a class may be one reason for this. Membership of a group may also create a useful spirit of competition, which stimulates learning.

Given the increasing pressure on university places in many countries, internet-based teaching is often seen as a convenient development. However, e-learning eliminates personal contact and travel from education, which are possibly the aspects many students value. Sitting at home working on a computer may be economical, but clearly cannot replace the social experience of attending courses. However, there are many people who are unable, either through work or family commitments, or due to lack of funds, to go to classes, and who would clearly find internet learning beneficial. On-line courses can also be used to support taught courses, for instance by providing access to extra materials. In many ways these kinds of courses are similar to 'universities of the air', such as Britain's Open University, which have developed distance learning so successfully in the last 40 years.

Faced by growing demand for university places, more institutions are likely to develop on-line courses, but the apparent benefits of e-learning may be less than are generally believed. Students seem to value the personal contact of the classroom highly, despite its cost and inconvenience. There may be a role for internet-based courses to supplement teacher-taught ones, and certainly for people with other commitments they will be the only practical option. There is an urgent need for research on the effectiveness of this type of learning, which should help maximise its advantages in the future.

(Approximately 550 words)

4.6 Discussion Essay

cross-reference
1.12   *Organising Paragraphs*
2.6   *Discussion*

1. **Read the essay carefully and then decide which of the headings below match each of the paragraphs 1–7.**

   A. The impact of education   E. Other factors

   B. Discussion/example   F. Introduction – definitions

   C. Introduction – aims and overview

   D. Conclusion   G. Limits of education

   ## EDUCATION IS THE MOST IMPORTANT FACTOR IN NATIONAL DEVELOPMENT – DISCUSS.

   1. Education must be considered on several different levels, so that today most Western countries are concerned with provision from nursery to higher education, while developing countries attempt to deliver basic education (e.g. reading and writing) to their people. 'National development' will be defined in this essay as the development of a country's economy, since this is most commonly seen as the function of education provided by the state. For example, many European countries began providing primary education for all citizens in the late nineteenth century, in the phase of early industrialisation.

   2. This paper attempts to evaluate the importance of these varying levels of educational provision in encouraging economic growth, compared to other factors such as national culture, natural resources and government. The role of education in fostering development will be examined first, and then other factors affecting growth will be considered.

   3. At its simplest, education sets out to teach literacy and numeracy. People who can read and count are capable of being trained for many roles in the industrial or service sectors, as well as learning by themselves. Even in the simplest economies, dependent on agriculture, the education of women has been shown to lead to dramatic improvements in family welfare. In more developed economies further skills are required, such as languages, engineering and computing. Good education does not merely teach people how to function passively, but provides them with the skills to ask questions and therefore make improvements. At university level, education is closely involved in research which leads to technical and social advances.

   4. Yet education does not operate in a vacuum: cultural, religious, legal and other factors all influence the rate of economic growth. Soviet Russia, for

example, had an advanced educational system, but many graduates were under-employed due to the restrictions of the political system. Similar situations exist in many countries today because of political restraints on the economy which prevent fast enough expansion to create sufficient jobs. Clearly, development requires efficient and honest government to encourage a dynamic economy.

5. A strong work ethic, as found in the USA or Japan, also aids growth. In such societies children are brought up to believe that both the individual and society will benefit from hard work. Natural resources such as oil are another consideration. Brunei, for instance, previously a poor country reliant on fishing, today has one of the highest per capita GDPs in the world. A clear and effective legal system also encourages development.

6. It is difficult to think of a situation where education has been the principal agent in fostering growth. For example, in the world's first industrial revolution, which occurred in eighteenth-century Britain, the majority of people were still illiterate (some pioneer industrialists themselves could not read or write). It seems that the availability of capital through the banking system, and a secure political and legal environment were more crucial in this case.

7. However, despite these considerations, education clearly has an important part to play in developing the skills and abilities of the people. Ultimately, they are the most important resource a country possesses, and their education is a priority for all successful states.

(Approximately 600 words)

cross-reference

3.7   Conjunctions

2. Underline all the conjunctions in the essay and list them in the table below.

Addition	Result	Reason	Time	Example	Opposition

Writing Tests

These tests can be used to assess different aspects of writing performance. The accuracy tests (1 and 3) check the use of particular word classes such as conjunctions or prepositions. Students having difficulties with, for example, articles, should look at the relevant unit in Part 3. The second test assesses cohesion and test 4 is a comparison. They can be used in the classroom or for self-assessment.

WRITING TEST 1

(Accuracy)

Read the text for gist and then complete it by writing **one** *word in each gap.*

Most overseas students who come to study
a) . . . . English-speaking countries find that
their first b) . . . . is listening. Understanding c)
. . . . many forms of spoken English is more d)
. . . . than they expected.

e) . . . ., after a month f) . . . . two, the
majority find that their listening g) . . . ., and their
next concern is speaking. This skill is more difficult to
practise, so improvement h) . . . . to be slower. But
i) . . . . three or four months most students find that
j) . . . . can function quite k) . . . . in terms of
shopping and travelling.

A l) . . . . area of difficulty is writing, which is
possibly the m) . . . . difficult skill to master,
n) . . . . it is more impersonal than oral/aural
skills and depends o) . . . . the student learning
a complex series of conventions. This explains p)
. . . . many students find it q) . . . . to attend
r) . . . . intensive course in academic English s)
. . . . they begin t) . . . . university studies.

WRITING TEST 2

(Cohesion)

The parts of sentences below make two paragraphs which compare speaking with writing. Some parts are already numbered. Fill in the remaining numbers. Use internal clues and punctuation to help you find the correct order.

SPEAKING AND WRITING

1) When we speak, it is normally to one or

. . .) to study our listeners' faces for expressions which tell

. . .) for example agreement, or amusement.

. . .) they often find the situation stressful.

3)   As we speak, we are able

. . .) For most people, speaking feels like a natural activity,

. . .) a small number of people, who are often well known to us.

. . .) If their expressions show incomprehension

. . .) us their reaction to what we are saying;

. . .) though if they have to make a formal speech

. . .) we will probably restate what we are saying.

. . .) Writers cannot check if the readers understand, or are interested

. . .) to avoid the dangers of being misunderstood by readers

. . .) who cannot look puzzled to

1)   Writing, however, is much more like speaking to

. . .) Unless we are writing a letter to a friend

. . .) This is the reason why writing is more difficult than

. . .) make the writer explain what he means again.

. . .) in what they are writing.

. . .) we have no way of knowing who may read our words.

. . .) It also explains why writing must be as clear and simple as possible,

. . .) speaking, and often uses a more formal style.

. . .) an unknown audience.

WRITING TEST 3

(Accuracy)

Read the text for gist and then complete it by writing one word in each gap.

All students need a) . . . . to live, so finding a suitable place is likely to be a priority when they arrive to start a new course. Apart b) . . . . the minority c) . . . . live with their parents, there are only two d) . . . . of accommodation which are generally affordable.

e) . . . . all universities provide f) . . . . of residence, which can help new students g) . . . . friends and develop a social life. They can be a h) . . . . choice, usually being close to other university facilities, i) . . . . some may find that they are noisy, expensive and have j) . . . . small rooms.

The alternative is to rent k) . . . . house or flat from a private landlord with a group of other students. l) . . . . kind of shared accommodation m) . . . . offer greater independence and privacy, and can n) . . . . be more economical. However, it does mean taking o) . . . . more responsibility, p) . . . . bills need paying and the rooms have to q) . . . . cleaned.

Wherever students choose to live, several things are r) . . . . A quiet place to work, a sense of security and s) . . . . environment that allows t) . . . . to sleep properly all contribute to academic success.

WRITING TEST 4

(Comparison)

Study the information in the table comparing two cities, which both have good universities. Use it to write a report on which would be the most suitable location for an overseas student planning a one-year course. (About 200 words.)

	Borchester	Rowborough
Population	220,000	1,560,000
Summer climate	Warm and wet	Cool and quite dry
Winter climate	Cool and windy	Cold and wet
City type	Old cathedral city with modern service industries	19th century industrial city with modern mixed industries
Terrain	Flat, lots of parks	Hilly with several lakes
Cost of accommodation	Quite high	Medium
Public transport	Bus service not very good	Buses and trams, both good
Main advantages	Relaxed atmosphere	Good range of shops and sports facilities
Main drawbacks	University campus is 6 kms from city centre	High rates of crime in some areas
Distance from capital	230 kms	125 kms

Answers

Part 1 – The Writing Process

1.1 Background to Writing

1

notes	to record reading or lectures	
report	to describe something a student has conducted, e.g. an experiment/a survey	1,000–2,000
project	research conducted either individually or in group on subject chosen by student(s)	1,000–3,000
essay	piece of writing used to assess coursework/subject chosen by teacher	1,000–5,000
thesis/dissertation	long piece of writing on subject chosen by student for final assessment in Master's/PhD course	30,000–70,000
article/paper	writing published in academic journal	5,000–10,000

2bi   abstract

2bii   acknowledgements

2biii   appendix

2biv   bibliography

2bv   case study

2bvi   preface

2bvii   index

4a   title

4b   sub-heading

4c   phrase

4d   sentence

4e   paragraph

5   Texts are divided into paragraphs to separate the main points and make them easier to read. Paragraphs usually vary in length from three to eight sentences.

     para 2 begins: The first issue to . . .

     para 3 begins: Diversification must also . . .

     para 4 begins: A further consideration . . .

1.2   Avoiding Plagiarism

1   (a), (b), (d) and (e) are plagiarism.

2   (a), (b) and (c) are plagiarised, (d) is acceptable.

NB (c) uses paraphrasing but contains a quotation not marked by quotation marks.

3   Acceptable: some vocabulary kept from original/new sentence structure/use of summary

Plagiarised: many phrases retained from original/minor paraphrasing/identical sentence structure

1.3   From Titles to Outlines

1a	Define	give a definition
	Outline	describe the main features
1b	Compare	examine the similarities
	Contrast	look at the differences
1c	Evaluate	consider the value
1d	Trace	describe the main features
	Illustrate	give examples
2	Describe	give a detailed account
	Examine	divide into sections and discuss each critically
	State	give a clear and simple account
	Suggest	make a proposal and support it
	Summarise	deal with a complex subject by giving the main points

4   (Sample plan)

Title	Evaluate the effects of mergers in the motor industry in the last ten years
Introduction	definition of *merger*
	background to motor industry
	outline of essay
Main body	case studies of two mergers
	discussion of benefits of each merger
Conclusion	summary of findings: value of mergers depends on quality of management in merged firm

5   The following sections are the most important:

5a   An analysis of candidates for membership before 2020/A summary of the enlargement of the EU from 1975 to now.

5b   A study of major privatisations in the UK/A discussion of the benefits achieved by privatisation.

5c A report on the spread of TB worldwide/A case study showing how TB relates to social class.

5d A report on the development of children who remain at home until five/A discussion comparing speaking ability in both groups of children.

5e The benefits of using books/The drawbacks of internet sources.

6a Identify means to select and explain. The writer must identify the chief reasons for poverty in the Chinese countryside.

6b Calculate means to make a mathematical estimate. Here the writer must look at patterns of coffee consumption and attempt to calculate how much difference a price decrease would make.

6c Classify means to put into categories. Different types of desert need to be described, and then methods of control should be proposed.

1.4 Evaluating Texts

2

a	opinion	
b	fact	false
c	fact	true
d	opinion	
e	fact	false
f	fact and opinion	

5a Factual and mainly true until last sentence (In the future . . .) which is an opinion.

5b Most sentences mix facts and opinions. Most of the facts are untrue, e.g. the population is not two million. Clearly an unreliable source!

5c Although this begins with a generally accepted fact, the second sentence contains a totally untrue statement, and the speculation built on this is absurd!

5d Mainly factual, except for an opinion in the first sentence (significant). The penultimate sentence is speculation.

1.5 Understanding Purpose and Register

2a amuse/entertain

2b inform/persuade

2c inform

3 Academic English is found in academic journals and books.

Archaic English is generally found in books published in the nineteenth century or earlier.

Formal English is found in legal documents and similar.

Jargon is often found in specialist publications.

Journalistic English is found in newspapers.

Literary English may be found in poems, plays and novels.

4a academic

4b formal

4c jargon

4d literary

4e archaic

4f journalistic

5a euphemism

5b metaphor

5c proverb

5d paradox

5e analogy

5f idiom

5g irony

5h hyperbole

6a (hyperbole) Obesity is a growing problem in modern society.

6b (irony) High consumption of sugar and fats contribute towards it.

6c (idiom) Overweight people should attempt to become fitter.

6d (idiom) They need to make the effort to take regular exercise.

6e (proverb) Ultimately, they need to take responsibility for their own health.

1.6   Selecting Key Points

2   Many possibilities, but should include the idea of financial success and medical developments, e.g. Millionaire American medical inventor.

3   1.   In many parts of the world hospitals have none of the modern health equipment . . .

2.   Freeplay Energy. . . is planning to introduce a range of medical equipment which can . . .

3.   All the machines will be of simple, robust design which will use either solar power . . .

4   1.   Lord May . . . has claimed that the world is facing a wave of extinctions similar to the five mass extinctions of past ages.

2.   He calculates that the current rate of extinction is between 100 and 1,000 times faster than the historical average.

3. . . . the present situation is caused by human consumption of plants, which has resulted in a steady increase in agriculture and a consequent reduction in habitat for animals.

4. Lord May also pointed out that it was very difficult to make accurate estimates as nobody knew how many species of animals lived on the planet.

5a . . . bottled water costs 700 times more than tap water, but is often of inferior quality.

. . . although bottled water advertising often associated the product with sport and health there was no truth in this link.

Labels on bottled water often referred to 'spring' and 'natural water', which were meaningless phrases.

5b Now the genetic code of the plague bacterium has been 'read' by scientists; a total of 465 million 'letters' of DNA. They believe that this will help in the development of vaccines for the plague . . .

1.7 Note-making

1 to keep a record of reading/lectures

to revise for exams

to help remember main points

to prepare for essays

2 Before: listening/reading/selecting

After: writing/speaking

3 Source: Lee, Y. (2005) *Computing Tomorrow* **15** pp. 134–7.

Computer passwords

generally used to protect sites from hackers

Drawbacks

a) office workers must remember av. 12 passwords ⟶ most use same one

b) many use simple words ⟶ hackers can easily crack

c) expense of supplying replacements for forgotten passwords

d) need to write down new passwords reduces security

Solutions

Passfaces (Real User)

a) user remembers set of photos of faces in order – selected from random pattern

b) works because people can recognise large number faces

c) more secure – cannot be passed on

d) more easily remembered

5   Source: Nemecova, I. (1998) *Medical Report* **34** pp. 78–86.

<u>Malaria increasing</u> esp. resistant strains

350 m+ cases p.a. (4× level 1970s)

Causes: a) increase in poverty > less money for sanitation

                    b) increased travel (migrants/tourists)

                    c) overuse of antibiotics

Vaccine? – difficult because of different strains but in trials

6   Source: Pitnam, E.B. (1993) *Volcanic Disasters* p. 221.

1815   Mt Tambora (Indonesia) exploded

        100 km³ debris ⟶ atmosphere ⟶ affected weather around world

1816   NE USA and Europe cold summers destroyed harvests > prices rose > more emigrants to west of USA

1.8   Paraphrasing

2   (b) is the better paraphrase (in (a) *changes in the weather* and *the region to the south* are not as precise as *a long dry period* and *the mountains at the river's source*).

4   (A number of possibilities are acceptable here. These are suggestions.)

4b   It *started* in France and Germany, but *accelerated* in the United States.

4c   There Henry Ford *modified* the moving *assembly* line from the Chicago meat industry to *car* manufacturing, *thereby* inventing mass production.

5b   After the Second World War the *development* of 'planned obsolescence' by the industry encouraged customers to buy new cars more often than they needed to by increasing the *frequency* of model changes.

5c   Later, from the 1970s, *environmental criticism* of the industry focused on the *production* of inefficient models which used too much fuel, contributing to global warming.

6b   Some of the strongest brands in the world are today owned by the industry.

6c   Many major car companies, however, struggle with falling profits and stagnant markets.

7   (Again, there is a range of possibilities, of which the following is an example.)

The expansion of contemporary capitalism matches the rise of the automobile industry. After starting in Germany and France, it accelerated in the United States. There the moving assembly line was modified by Henry Ford from the Chicago meat industry to manufacturing cars: the invention of mass production. General Motors dominated the world's car companies in the 1920s, with help from the managerial theories of Alfred Sloan. The development of 'planned obsolescence' by the industry began after the Second World War, by which the frequency of model changes encouraged customers to buy new cars more often than necessary. Environmental criticism of the industry from the 1970s focused on the contribution to global warming made by the production of inefficient models which used too much petrol. At this time increasingly militant trades unions defended their members' jobs. Although some of the world's strongest brands are today owned by the industry, many major motor companies struggle with declining profits and static markets.

8.   (Sample paraphrase)

Antarctica was unexplored until the twentieth century, and still has a tiny population in relation to its size. Yet it suffers from various pollution problems which have been described in a report by a New Zealand government agency. The low temperatures there impede the usual pattern of decay, though compared with most parts of the world it remains in pristine condition. Some long-established scientific bases have large piles of garbage around them.

Few people realise that Antarctica has very little precipitation, so that in the current context of global warming the ice tends to reveal the rubbish that previously was slowly being buried under snow. For more than a decade the nations involved in Antarctic research have respected an agreement to repatriate their garbage, and this should gradually solve the problem. But there are a few items which will not be cleared up, since they belonged to the early period of exploration and have now acquired historic interest.

1.9   Summary Writing

1   Features of good summaries should include: selection of main features/accuracy (i.e. not distorting the original)/clear expression.

2   making detailed notes from sections of journal articles and books

making global summaries of writers' ideas and theses

3

3b   key points

3c   use your own words

3d   order of ideas where necessary

3e   important points

4   (a) is the best summary

(b) fails to describe the experiment

(c) describes neither the experiment nor its significance

6   (Possible answers)

6a   weather forecasting methods

6b   blossoming of local tree

6c   castor (for dry)

6d   the monsoon can be quite accurately forecast by the time of the tree's flowering

7   Model answer

Indian scientists are checking ancient weather forecasting methods, such as the old saying which links the date of the monsoon to the flowering time of a local tree. This has been used by farmers to select either peanuts (for wet conditions) or castor (for dry). Dr Kanani of Gujarat Agricultural University has found that the monsoon can be quite accurately forecast using the time of the tree's flowering.

8   Model answer

Recent Indian research confirms the accuracy of an ancient method of forecasting the monsoon's arrival used by farmers to choose crops.

9   Model answer

It is planned to move South Korea's capital from Seoul to a central site by 2012, at a cost of $45 billion. Although Seoul is crowded and too near the border, critics claim that this scheme will be too expensive and take too long. Businesses are unlikely to move away from Seoul when the government does. Other countries have experienced severe problems with capital relocation.

1.10 Combining Sources

1a   4

1b   to introduce summaries

1c   Others, however,

3a   direct quote: 'such procedures are now labelled "interfering with nature"'

summary: GM techniques are no different from breeding techniques which have been practised by man for thousands of years.

3b   On the other hand

3c   Source A states that

Source B considers that

He believes that

4   Model answer

Source C claims that tourism creates a significant amount of employment which provides a welcome alternative to traditional work such as farming. However, source D points out that many of these jobs are insecure and poorly paid, being likely to contribute to social tensions. This negative view is partly supported by source E, who insists that despite some positive examples the more common experience of developing countries is for tourism to exacerbate social ills such as crime and prostitution.

1.11 Planning Essays

1   Other possible ideas: tourism helps poorer countries develop

pressure to offer 'new' countries

tourist industry vulnerable to political/natural disasters

package holidays helped to popularise foreign travel

huge potential demand from developing countries

2   Most suitable structure would be based on time, since the title asks for study of past and present.

3   (Sample plan)

Main body: ii)   package holidays helped to popularise foreign travel

iii) tourism helped poorer countries to develop

iv) constant demand for new destinations and new types of holiday

v)   danger of damaging environment through growth of visitors

Conclusion: industry has grown rapidly but faces variety of threats

4a   For and against

4b   Comparison

4c   Time

4d   For and against

4e   Comparison

5   Main body: i)   benefits of TV advertising: reach large audience, have strong impact

ii)   drawbacks: expensive and can be ignored

iii) benefits of newspaper advertising: flexible, cheap, focused

iv) drawbacks: static

Conclusion: TV more effective in reaching large numbers but newspapers probably better for specialised markets

7   Introduction

- In 1985 12% of young people went to university in the UK. Now the figure is over 30%. Similar growth has been experienced in many countries, developed and developing.

- Outline of essay: benefits and drawbacks of expansion.

Main body

1.   Benefits of expansion

- Modern economies are based on knowledge. Therefore, every country needs to educate its workforce as highly as possible to compete with other economies.

- University education may help students from poorer families to move into a higher social position.

2. Drawbacks of expansion

- As student numbers rise, standards fall. Classrooms become more crowded, and overworked teachers are less able to give students personal attention.

- Because increasing numbers of young people are gaining a first degree, their degrees are worth less. It is now necessary to have a second degree to compete in the labour market.

- Recent research (Jackson *et al.*) shows that employers are looking for personal skills rather than educational qualifications.

- The average student in Britain now leaves university with debts of £15,000.

3. Discussion

Higher education does not benefit everyone. Advantages have to be balanced against time and money invested.

4. Conclusion

Not clear that numbers in higher education can be expanded indefinitely.

1.12 Organising paragraphs

3   1. Topic

2. Definition

3. Example

4. Detail

5. Detail

6. Reason

4   Topic: London has been . . .

Restatement: For many centuries . . .

Reason: Its dominance is due . . .

Example: The Romans were the first . . .

Information: Over 500 years ago . . .

5   1. Topic 1: An English zoo . . .

2. Topic 2: But when the English . . .

3. Example: Even simple words . . .

4. Reason: The zoo realised that . . .

5. Information: Consequently, the keepers . . .

Model answers for (6–9)

6 1. . . . was developed in the 19th century.

   2. . . . to isolate, punish and reform.

   3. . . . there has been a steep rise in the number of prisoners.

   4. . . . as being 'universities of crime'.

   5. . . . how effective prisons are today.

7 1. Prisons appear to offer society three benefits.

   2. Firstly, they punish prisoners by depriving them of freedom.

   3. In addition, offenders are segregated from society so they cannot commit further crimes.

   4. Finally, they offer the possibility of reform through training programmes.

8 1. Prisons, however, appear to many observers to be failing in the twenty-first century.

   2. In most countries the prison population is rising steadily.

   3. Furthermore, many prisoners return to prison after their release; they are repeat offenders.

   4. This suggests that few prisons offer effective reform programmes.

   5. In addition, prison conditions can often be brutal and degrading.

9 Prisons have existed in their present form for about 200 years and are clearly necessary to deter and punish criminals. However, they are often no longer successful in this aim, as shown by the steady increase in the prison population, and the rise of re-offending. It would appear that more emphasis should be placed on reform and education, as well as examining alternatives to prison, such as community work.

1.13 Organising the Main Body

1a For and against/type 1

1b Comparison

1c Development

2 Structure: For and against/type 1

   1. many older students have lost interest in learning and disrupt classes

   2. problem students waste everybody's time, including their own

   3. some students are more suited to work which doesn't require qualifications

   4. in future, almost all jobs will require academic skills

   5. if they left at 14, students would be unlikely to find proper jobs

   6. effort should be made in primary schools to prevent pupils falling behind

3   1.   Literature review – A synopsis of recent published research in this area

    2.   Aims and methods – Aims of the survey and how the researcher conducted it

    3.   Findings – A report of what the survey found, with statistical analysis

    4.   Case study – An extensive study of two students . . .

    5.   Discussion – Comparisons of the advantages and disadvantages that students mentioned . . .

5   (Possible answers)

    Para 2   The main factor

            In the first place

            Then

            Finally,

    Para 3   Turning to the subject of

            In the first place

            Secondly

            Lastly,

    Para 4   Another important area

            Firstly

            in addition

1.14 Introductions

1   optional: a/c

    usual: d/e/g

2a   v

2b   i

2c   iv

2d   vi

2e   ii

2f   iii

4a   Higher Education

4b   depending on the country chosen, recent developments/debate on HE could be mentioned

4c   reference could be made to rising student numbers/debate about costs (who should pay)/value of research for economic development

4d   essay could focus geographically on one or two countries, either similar or different economically historically the discussion could be limited to the past 10/20/50 years

4e plan will depend on decisions made in (c) above

5 Model answer

The last two decades have seen a steady increase in demand for higher (i.e. university-level) education worldwide. Rising costs in this sector have put pressure on national budgets, causing many countries to attempt to shift some of the cost to the students, often in the form of loans. A degree generally remains the key to better jobs and opportunities, yet if students have to pay a greater share of the cost this will discriminate against poorer families. This essay examines the question of access to university by comparing the situation in a developed country, the United States, with that of a developing country, Turkey.

1.15 Conclusions

1a ii

1b iii

1c v

1d iv

1e ii

1f i

1g ii

1h iv

2 Neither conclusion is complete – synthesis is required

2a Summary of discussion/reference to related research

2b Limitations of study/proposals for future research

3 (Suggested order – variations possible)

Summary of main findings

Reference to how these findings compare with other studies *or* Implications of the findings

Limitations of research

Proposals for further research

4 Model answer

Summary: The results suggest that culture was only one factor in determining successful adaptation. Older students, those with previous experience of living abroad, and those with better language proficiency all seemed to adapt better.

Implications: The findings suggest that students should if possible study abroad when they are more mature, and that they should aim for a higher level of language ability before they leave home.

Limitations: Although this was quite a large survey only about 30% of overseas students at the university were involved. Some national groups were under-represented.

Proposals: As we are not aware of other previous research in this field, it would be useful to replicate the study in another university, possibly with a different cross-section of overseas students, to see if similar results emerged.

5   Model answer

It has been shown that despite the distinct benefits that on-line learning can bring, especially cheapness and flexibility, these are not always sufficient to dissuade students from attending classroom lessons. They clearly value membership of a group and personal contact with a teacher. There is a sense that internet teaching may be seen as second-class education, where the student is isolated from fruitful contact with his or her peers, and a more useful approach may be to view e-learning as a helpful add-on to taught courses, rather than an avenue to be followed exclusively.

1.16 Rewriting and Proof-reading

4   Model answer

Despite this, there are significant differences between the structure and workings of the higher education system in the two countries. This essay attempts to compare the admission procedures, length of courses for first and higher degrees, teaching methods, assessment procedures and systems of financial support for students. These areas have been selected as being of central importance for a valid comparison.

5a   v

5b   iv

5c   vii

5d   ii

5e   x

5f   vi

5g   i

5h   ix

5i   iii

5j   viii

6a   *50 years*

6b   *its* citizens/contribute *to*

6c   *teaches* people/ knowledge

6d   *whether* it is

6e   There *was*

6f   depends *on/educational* level

6g   the *highest*

7   (Corrected sections in italics)

There are many *similarities between* the UK and Taiwan, for example course fees *and* assessment. Firstly, both UK and *Taiwanese* universities charge fees *to* students, *and* course fees in the UK *are* as expensive as *those* in *Taiwan*. In addition, teaching methods are very similar *in* both countries: students *have to* attend lectures and seminars. *Moreover*, they have the same system to assess students, *who* are *examined* at the end of *each* semester. Nevertheless, there are *two* main differences: how students can *enter* a university and *what* percentage of students are in higher education. *There are twice as many students in higher education in Taiwan as in the UK.*

Part 2 – Elements of Writing

2.1   Argument

3   Problem: Obesity is increasing rapidly in most countries.

Cause A: . . . some doctors blame a sedentary lifestyle.

Argument against cause A: This does not explain why only certain people suffer from this condition . . .

Cause B: Another theory is that a high-fat diet . . . is to blame.

Conclusion in favour of B: Recent research has shown that most obesity sufferers do eat this unhealthy diet.

4   Model argument

Demand for university places is currently growing, which frequently leads to overcrowding of student facilities. It has been argued that fees should be increased to reduce demand for places, but this would discriminate against students from poorer families. Another proposal is for the government to pay for the expansion of universities, but against this is the view that this would unfairly benefit the minority who in any case go on to earn higher salaries. A fairer solution might be for the government to subsidise the fees of the poorest students.

2.2   Cause and Effect

3a   leads to/results in

3b   Because of/Owing to/Due to

3c   leads to/causes/results in/produces

3d   therefore/consequently/which is why

3e   led to/resulted in

4a   because of/due to/owing to

4b   because/since

4c   consequently/therefore

4d   due to/owing to/because of

4e   because of/due to/owing to

4f   so/therefore/thus/consequently

5   Model answer

This results in people having more money to spend, and so leads to higher spending on goods and services. The increased demand for goods and services results in lower unemployment, and consequently the government has a higher income from taxation and spends less on social security.

2.3   Cohesion

2   they

this

the former

the latter

these

3   villagers

kerosene and diesel

not being affordable

villagers

kerosene and diesel

from kerosene and diesel

4a   They

4b   he

4c   them

4d   This

4e   his

4f   he

5A   a   It

5A   b   her

5A   c   She

5A   d   him

5A   e   They/She

5A   f   Their

5A g   she

5A h   his

5B a   Their

5B b   their

5B c   They

5B d   their

5B e   Their

5B f   the former

2.4   Comparisons

3a   slightly more expensive than

3b   considerably/significantly cheaper than

3c   slightly cheaper than

3d   considerably/significantly more expensive than

7a   least

7b   slightly

7c   nearly/almost

7d   as

7e   most

7f   than

7g   half

7h   as

8a   most

8b   less

8c   more

8d   than

8e   slightly

8f   on

8g   as

8h   smallest/least

9a   shows

9b   longest/highest

9c   longest

9d   On

9e   than

9f   the

9g   slightly

10. Model answer

The highest rate is found in Greece (8.3 per day), and the lowest is in Norway (1.7). Although many countries are close to the EU average of 4.5, the northern Scandinavian countries all have low rates of smoking.

11. Model answer

Alcohol consumption in Europe averages 11.1 litres per adult per year, but within this there are wide variations. The highest consumption is found in France (14.1), while the Norwegians only consume one third of this figure (4.8).

2.5   Definitions

2a   instrument/device

2b   organs

2c   organisation/corporation

2d   material

2e   behaviour

2f   system/process

2g   period/time

2h   system

3a	process	refine liquids
3b	person/doctor	mental problems
3c	qualification/degree	a dissertation/thesis
3d	body/organisation	its members' interests
3e	disease	a mosquito-borne parasite
3f	cereal/grain	making flour

4a   a failed project

4b   development

4c   electronic commerce

4d   attachment

4e   self-brightening

Model answers

5a	capital punishment	execution carried out by state, often by hanging

5b department store   large shop which sells most types of goods in different areas

5c post-natal depression   feeling of sadness experienced by some mothers after birth

2.6 Discussion

3 Model answer for title (a)

pros: more security for children with mother, mother is able to take more care of home

cons: children have less chance to mix with others, mothers have more limited role

Title: Instead of going out to work, mothers should stay at home and look after their children until they are at least 5 – discuss.

a) Introduction   the growth in women's participation in the workforce
                     – increased use of nurseries

b) Advantages   more social mixing for children

                     higher income for family

                     more varied roles for women

c) Disadvantages   less security for children

                     women have to deal with career and home

d) Conclusion   depends on individual situation

5 Model answers

It has been argued that staying at home gives children security, but the evidence suggests that there are more social advantages to attending a nursery.

While fast food is often claimed to be unhealthy, there appears to be little firm evidence to support this.

7 Model answer

Lomborg's definition of air quality is limited to sulphur dioxide, and fails to take into account more recent threats.

8 Model answer

pros: increases standard of living, reduces time spent working, people live longer

cons: creates pollution, damages environment, causes stress and mental problems

9 Model answer using pattern (2i)

a) Introduction: definition of industrial development, examples of process

b) Advantages: more leisure time, better medical facilities, more choices

c) Disadvantages: development destroys countryside, causes pollution and stress

d) Discussion/conclusion: quality of life has improved due to industrialisation but damage has been caused on several levels

2.7   Examples

2a   e.g./such as

2b   A case in point

2c   particularly/especially (for example/instance also possible)

2d   for instance/for example

2e   such as/e.g.

Model answers

3a   A number of sports such as football/motor racing . . .

3b   Certain twentieth-century inventions, for example television and antibiotics, . . .

3c   In recent years many women, e.g. Indira Gandhi . . .

3d   . . . most car makers, for instance Toyota/Volkswagen . . .

3e   Certain diseases, particularly malaria/Aids . . .

3f   Many musical instruments such as guitars/violins . . .

3g   Several mammals, e.g. pandas/tigers . . .

4   customs: holidays and festivals, ways of greeting people

everyday patterns: types of shop, shop opening times

inevitable differences: language, currency

rapid changes of mood: depression, elation

relatively short period: two/three months

some aspects of their new surroundings: freedom, independence

5a   His mother's sister, i.e. his aunt . . .

5b   When the liquid reached boiling point, namely 140 degrees . . .

5c   It appears that Candlemas day, that is, February 2nd, . . .

5d   The company's overheads, in other words, the fixed costs, . . .

2.8   Generalisations

Model answers

2b   Flowers are usually a suitable present.

2c   Cities are often affected by pollution.

2d   Fresh fruit can be good for health.

2e   Television has become an important medium.

3   Many international students attend British universities. Most welcome the chance to meet students from around the world, and all are pleased to have a chance to improve their English.

4a   Unemployment in 1989 was higher than in 1979 or 1999.

4b   Inflation was higher in 1979 than in 1989 or 1999.

4c   House prices rose dramatically between 1979 and 1989.

4d   Interest rates were slightly higher in 1989 than in 1979, and were much lower in 1999.

5a   be over 60

5b   double by 2100

5c   young populations/a small proportion of over-60s

5d   fall in its total population/a doubling of the population over 60

5e   have a significant population of older people/a larger proportion of over 60s

Model answers

6a   Two common dreams are being chased and falling.

6b   A majority have dreamed about the dead.

6c   Dreaming about the future is quite common.

6d   Food dreams may be linked to dieting.

6e   A minority dream of finding money.

2.9   Numbers

2a   50

2b   100

2c   400

3a   Few people . . .

3b   They received scores . . .

3c   She made various . . .

3d   He found dozens . . .

3e   They made several. . .

Model answers

4a   Three quarters of the people interviewed said that they supported the president.

4b   The average number of students on the course has been 22.

4c   The price of petrol has increased eight times/eightfold since 1965.

4d   Two thirds of the students in the group were women.

4e   The new type of train halved the journey time to Madrid.

4f   The majority of the students studied law.

4g   There has been a 50% rise in the numbers applying to this department this year.

5b   The numbers doubled every year between 1998 and 2000.

5c   More than twice as many students complete their first degree course in Britain, compared with Italy.

5d   Tap water is much cheaper than bottled water.

5e   Only a small percentage/proportion of women believed that they had the same rights as men. Over a third complained that they had far fewer rights.

5f   Life expectancy for men in the UK rose by 50% during the twentieth century.

5g   The cost of the same operation varies by 50% between hospitals in . . .

5h   The area of forest in England fell by two-thirds between 1086 and 1870.

2.10 Opening Paragraphs

2   Model answer

It is now widely accepted that global warming, caused by increased use of fossils fuels, is taking place. The debate now centres on the best approach to the phenomenon. Some scientists argue for a reduction in the use of fossil fuels, but others maintain that this is impractical or uneconomic.

3a   acceptable

3b   too vague

3c   acceptable

3d   vague and overgeneralised

5   Model answer

a)   In the past 50 years television has become one of the dominant influences on the upbringing of children. Most children watch it, and many spend several hours daily watching programmes specially made for children. There are, however, concerns that children are watching unsuitable programmes, and also that they are spending too long in front of the television and not taking part in more productive activities.

2.11 References and Quotations

2   (a), (d) and (e) need references

5   Model answers

5a   Orwell (1940) stated that Dickens rarely writes directly about work. He claimed that most of Dickens' characters, except David Copperfield, have shadowy occupations, and that Copperfield works in areas very similar to Dickens' own experience.

5b   Orwell pointed out that Dickens infrequently described his characters' jobs clearly: 'In Dickens' novels anything in the nature of work happens off-stage. The only one of his heroes who has a plausible profession is David Copperfield . . . .' (Orwell, 1940: pp. 54–5)

5c According to Orwell (1940), few of Dickens' characters have a convincing profession, with the exception of David Copperfield, who follows Dickens' own career. 'With most of the others, the way they earn their living is very much in the background.' (pp. 54–5)

8a alphabetically

8b i   author/date of publication/title/place of publication/publisher

8b ii   author/date of publication/title/editor/main title/place of publication/publisher

8b iii author/title/URL/access date

8b iv   author/article title/journal name/volume/page number

8c book and journal titles

8d for titles of books (but not articles)

8e under the title of the publication

2.12 Restatement and Repetition

2a In other words, this may lead to . . .

2b . . . universities, i.e. coursework and examinations

2c That is to say, the distribution of wealth . . .

4a Every country has a unique structure for its education system.

4b Similarly, China has expanded its higher education.

4c There are two differences between the UK and China in terms of higher education. Firstly, the entrance system.

4d In Spain only 40% of students can find a job.

4e Students who graduate from secondary schools can send application forms to many universities.

4f Both UK and Chinese universities charge fees.

4g This essay will compare HE systems in the UK and China. Firstly, there are similar assessment methods.

5a a/c

5b d/e

5c b

5d g

6   Currently, fast food is growing in popularity. Fast food is food that people can buy or cook quickly. This essay examines the advantages and drawbacks of fast food. First, it is usually tasty. Most people who work in offices are very busy, so they do not have time to go home for lunch. But they can eat in McDonald's restaurants. The second benefit of fast food is cheapness. As it is produced in large quantities, this means that the companies can keep costs down. As a result fast food is usually less expensive than a meal in a conventional restaurant.

2.13 Academic Style

Model answers

4a   It is widely believed that the railways are deteriorating.

4b   Serious crime, such as murder, is increasing.

4c   The figures in that report are not reliable.

4d   The second factor is that the majority of children in that district may become criminals.

4e   There appears to be a significant risk of further strikes and disorder.

4f   Women were enfranchised in 1994.

4g   The Russian inflation led to poverty and disease.

4h   A malaria vaccine may be discovered in the next 10 years.

4i   There were two main causes of the American Revolution.

5a   Currently, significant numbers of children are starting school at the age of four or less, whereas 30 years ago five was the normal age. There appear to be various reasons for the change; mothers, for example, need to rejoin the labour force. There are mixed views about the effects of this change on the children concerned. Jenkins (1989) claims that early school attendance causes social problems such as theft and drug taking. There seems to be considerable evidence to support his views and there may be an argument in favour of a state subsidy for women to stay at home with their children.

5b   There appear to be two principal reasons for the growing traffic congestion. Firstly, public transport has become increasingly expensive relative to the falling cost of motoring. In addition, car ownership is much more convenient than using public transport. Together, these factors result in higher vehicle density.

2.14 Synonyms

Model answers

4a   challenged/outcome/study

4b   data *or* figures/demonstrate/increase

4c   forecast/argument *or* debate

4d   main disadvantage/method

4e   focus/possibility

4f   explain/idea *or* theory

4g   topics/evaluated

4h   structure/kept/targets/changed

4i   reduce output/increase

4j   tendency/accelerated

5   UK – British – this country

agency – organisation – body

advertising campaign – publicity programme – advertising blitz

to raise – to improve

British eating habits – regular hand washing

to cut – reduction

6   firm's plan

cut expenditure *or* spending

business intends *or* proposes

earnings *or* salaries

employees

raised

2.15 Variation in Sentence Length

Model answers

2   Worldwide, enrolments in higher education are increasing. In developed countries over half of all young people enter college, while similar trends are seen in China and South America. This growth has put financial strain on state university systems, so that many countries are asking students and parents to contribute. This leads to a debate about whether students or society benefit from tertiary education.

3   It is widely recognised that a university degree benefits the individual, since a graduate can expect to find a better job with a higher salary. In the USA the average graduate will earn $1 million more in a lifetime than a non-graduate. Many governments now expect students to pay a proportion of tuition costs, although it is argued that this discriminates against poorer students. Some countries give grants to students whose families have low incomes because their education is seen to be beneficial for the nation as a whole.

4   China is one developing country (but not the only one) which has imposed fees on students since 1997. The results have been surprising: enrolments, especially in the most expensive universities, have continued to rise steeply, growing 200% overall between 1997 and 2001. It seems in this case that higher fees attract rather than discourage students, who see them as a sign of a good education. They compete more fiercely for places, leading to the result that a place at a good college can cost $8000 per year for fees and maintenance.

5   Developing countries are under the greatest financial pressure. They may also experience difficulties in introducing loan schemes for students, since the lack of private capital markets restricts the source of borrowing for governments, which are often unable to raise sufficient cheap funds, while a further restraint has been the high default rates by students unable to repay their loans.

2.16 Visual Information

1.1 dE

1.2 fB

1.3 aF

1.4 cC

1.5 bD

1.6 eA

Model answers

2a   grew slightly

2b   rose steadily

2c   fell sharply

2d   increased slightly

2e   sharp rise

2f   slight drop

3   (a) is better because it selects the most important details. (b) simply repeats the data on the chart.

Model answers

4a   density

4b   illustrates/shows

4c   between

4d   emptier/less crowded

4e   role/part

4f   since/because

4g   tend

5a   table

5b   range/variety

5c   marriage

5d   Britain

5e   rate

5f   Iran

5g   half

5h   proportion/figure

5i   result/consequence

7   Model answer

Table 4 shows the gender balance in the School of Computing from 1996 to 2000. Between 1996 and 1998 the ratio of men to women was about 1:3, but in the next two years the proportion of women increased, so that in 2000 women accounted for nearly 40% of the total.

Part 3 – Accuracy In Writing

3.1   Abbreviations

6a   Prime Minister/members of parliament/National Health Service

6b   Information technology/and others

6c   That is/World Trade Organization

6d   Take note/Curricula vitarum/A4 size paper

6e   Organization for Economic Co-operation and Development/United Kingdom

6f   European Union/value added tax

6g   Chief Executive Officer/research and development

6h   Figure 4/Worldwide Web

6i   World Health Organization/tuberculosis

6j   Public Relations/$45,000

6k   Genetically modified/for example

6l   Professor/Master of Philosophy/Doctor of Philosophy

3.2   Academic Vocabulary

2a   prediction

2b   significant

2c   varied

2d   created

2e   hypothetical

2f   synthesis

2g   significance

2h   evaluated

2i   correlation

2j   analytical

3a   indicate

3b   definitive

3c   generalisations/predictions

3d   responded

3e   analysed

3f   variables

5a   precise

5b   theoretical

5c   irrational

5d   approximate

5e   objective

5f   irrelevant

5g   concrete

3.3   Adverbs

4a   Obviously/Clearly

4b   Originally

4c   Alternatively

4d   Recently/lately

4e   Similarly

4f   Clearly/Obviously

6a   slightly

6b   substantially/significantly

6c   dramatically

6d   steadily

6e   considerably/substantially/significantly

6f   rapidly/quickly

6g   substantially/considerably

6h   rapidly

3.4   Articles

4a   –

4b   The/the

4c   –/–

4d   The/the

4e   –/the

4f   –/the

4g   The/the

4h   The/–

4i   –/the

4j   The/the

4k   the/–

4l   The/–

4m   the/the

4n   The/the

5a   a

5b   –

5c   the

5d   the

5e   the/a

5f   the

5g   the

5h   a

5i   the

5j   the

5k   the

5l   a

5m   a

5n   The

5o   the

5p   –

5q   The

5r   the

5s   the/a

5t   the

5u   the

5v   the

5w   the

5x   a

5y   the

3.5   Caution

2   (Others are possible)

Modals: might/may/could/should

Adverbs: often/usually/frequently/generally/occasionally/rarely/mainly

Phrases: in general/by and large/it appears/it seems

3   Model answers

3a   Private companies tend to be . . .

3b   Computer manuals can be . . .

3c   Older students frequently perform better . . .

3d   Exploring space could be . . .

3e   English pronunciation is often . . .

3f   Global warming may cause . . .

3g   Science students tend to work harder . . .

3h   Concrete is usually . . .

4a   Charles was a rather insignificant king . . .

4b   The survey was quite a comprehensive . . .

4c   His second book had a rather hostile . . .

4d   . . . arthritis drugs are fairly expensive.

4e   The first-year students were quite fascinated . . .

6   Model answer

A team of American scientists *may* have found a way to reverse the ageing process. They fed diet supplements, *usually* found in health food shops, to elderly rats, which were then tested for memory and stamina. The animals *tended to* display more active behaviour after taking the supplements, and *generally* their memory improved. In addition, their appearance became *rather* more youthful and their appetite increased.

The researchers *believe* that this experiment is *quite* a clear indication of how the problems of old age *may* be overcome. They *claim* that in a few years' time *many people may* be able to look forward to a *fairly* long and active retirement.

3.6 Confusing Pairs

2a   quite

2b   lose

2c   affect

2d   compliments

2e   its

2f   economic

2g   accepted

3   (Others are correct)

3c   economical

3d   principles

3e   Except

3h   raise

3.7 Conjunctions

2a   d

2b   c

2c   f

2d   e

2e   a

2f   b

2g   b

2h   e

4   because (reason)

    for example (example)

    and (addition)

    But (opposition)

    so (result)

    while (addition)

    Firstly (time)

    and (addition)

    furthermore (addition)

5   (Others are possible)

Addition: moreover/as well as/in addition/and/also

Result: therefore/consequently/so/that is why

Reason: because/owing to/as a result of/as/since

Time: after/while/then/next/subsequently

Example: such as/e.g./in particular

Opposition: but/yet/while/however/nevertheless/whereas

6   (Other answers possible)

6a   Although

6b   i.e./namely

6c   After

6d   Although/While

6e   moreover/furthermore

6f   so/therefore

6g   for instance

6h   Because of/Due to

6i   Secondly/Subsequently

6j   While

7a   After

7b   Despite/In spite of

7c   such as

7d   In addition/Furthermore

7e   then/later

7f   while

7g   Because of/Due to

7h   although/though

7i   since/because/as

7j   and

7k   However

7l   so

7m   finally

8a   While the government claimed that inflation was falling, the opposition said it was rising.

Despite the fact that the government claimed (that) inflation was falling, the opposition . . .

8b This department must reduce expenditure, but it needs to install new computers.

Although this department must reduce expenditure it needs . . .

Model answers

9a In contrast to America, where gun ownership is common, guns are rare in Japan.

9b Despite leaving school at the age of 14 he went on to own a chain of shops.

9c The majority displayed a positive attitude to the proposal, but a minority rejected it.

9d While the tutor insisted that the essay was easy, the students felt it was too difficult.

9e Although the spring was cold and dry the summer was warm and wet.

3.8 Nationality Language

3 Model answer

Mexico is in central America.

The Mexican capital is Mexico City.

Mexicans speak Spanish.

5a Chinese

5b Russian

5c Australia

5d Spanish

5e American

5f Brazilians

5g Iraqi

5h Cubans

6 Model answers

Pablo Picasso came from Spain and painted pictures.

Bob Marley was a Jamaican musician.

Mahatma Gandhi was an Indian politician and philosopher.

3.9 Nouns and Adjectives

2a safety – safe

2b culture – cultural

2c deep – depth

2d health – healthy

3 high/reliable/hot

    strength/confidence/truth

    wide/probable/necessary

    length/danger/relevance

4a strength

4b truth

4c probability

4d wide

4e necessary

4f relevance

4g danger

4h necessity

4i unreliable

4j Confidence

5a various – variety

5b analytical – analysis

5c available – availability

5d major – majority

5e precise – precision/unknown – knowledge

5f theoretical – theory

5g frequent – frequency

5h critical – criticism *or* critic

5i Social – society

5j practical – practice

6   approximation/particularity

    superior/reasonable

    strategy/synthesis

    political/economic + economical

    industry/culture

    external/average

7a economic

    approximation

    particularity

    external

synthesis

average

reasonable

culture

3.10 Nouns – Countable and Uncountable

4   Model answers

4a   . . . of teaching is required

4b   . . . travelling in the desert

4c   . . . insufficient capital

4d   . . . during a meal

4e   . . . mainly political centres

4f   . . . are moved around the world daily

4g   . . . huge loss of life

4h   . . . many great films

4i   Her carelessness . . .

4j   . . . a great leveller

4k   . . . in those laboratories

4l   . . . very demanding

5a   Little

5b   businesses

5c   experience/is

5d   travel broadens

5e   Paper was

5f   much advice

5g   few interests

5h   war

5i   Irons were

5j   behaviour

6a   little

6b   much

6c   many

6d   few

6e   little

3.11   Nouns – Umbrella

1a   cause

1b   theory

1c   event

1d   feature

1e   machine

1f   area

1g   organisation

1h   views

1i   consideration

1j   process

1k   types

1l   problem

2a   body

2b   phenomenon

2c   issues

2d   field

2e   device

2f   concept

2g   aspects

2h   categories

2i   concern

2j   factor

2k   perspectives

3.12   Prefixes and Suffixes

3

    auto   by itself

    co   together

    ex   (i) previous

             (ii) outside

micro	small
multi	many
over	too much
post	later
re	again
sub	below
under	(i) below
	(ii) not enough

4a   social class at bottom of society

4b   more tickets sold than seats available

4c   very local climate

4d   economy based on information not production

4e   not listed in the telephone book

4f   disappointed

8a   noun – something which is no longer offered

8b   adjective – two related events at the same time

8c   adverb – without cooperation

8d   adjective – related to evolution

8e   noun – person who protests

8f   adjective – not able to be forecast

8g   adjective – able to be sold

8h   noun – person being interviewed

8i   noun – style of ultra-realistic painting

8j   adverb – in a way that suggests a symbol

9a   joint production/junior company

9b   without choosing to/not hurt

9c   able to be refilled/certain

9d   cannot be provided/unusual

9e   existing in theory/breaking into pieces

3.13 Prepositions

1.   purpose *of*/development *of*/*in* Britain/*over* the period/contributed *to*/valuable *for*/*In* conclusion/sets *out*/relationship *between*/decline *in*/supply *of*/*in* the factory

Verb + = contributed to

Adj .+ = valuable for

Phrasal verb = sets out

Place = in Britain/factory

Time = over the period

Phrase = In conclusion

2b adjective +

2c verb +

2d place

2e noun +

2f phrase

2g place

2h time

3a of

3b in

3c of

3d for

3e of

3f on

4a On

4b of

4c of

4d In

4e of

4f On

4g In

4h of

5a Among

5b from/to

5c in/of

5d in/in

5e in/at

5f On/between

6a out

6b   of

6c   in/to

6d   to

6e   among/in

6f   from

6g   between

6h   in

6i   of

6j   over

6k   between

6l   in

6m   in

6n   of

6o   in/to

3.14 Punctuation

7a   On Tuesday June 6, 1759, in the church at Derby, Nicolas James married Mary Dewey.

7b   Professor Rowan's new book, *The Triumph of Capitalism*, is published in New York.

7c   How many people would agree with John Lennon when he said: 'All You Need is Love'?

7d   The probability was calculated for each of the three faculties: Physics, Biology and Law.

7e   As Cammack (1994) points out: 'Latin America is creating a new phenomenon: democracy without citizens.'

7f   Thousands of new words such as 'website' enter the English language each year.

7g   Dr Tanner's latest study focuses on children's reactions to stress in the playground.

7h   She scored 56% on the main course; the previous semester she had achieved 67%.

8   The London School of Business is offering three new courses this year: Economics with Psychology; Introduction to Management; and e-commerce. The first is taught by Dr Jennifer Hillary and runs from October to January. The second, Introduction to Management, for MSc Finance students, is offered in the second semester, and is assessed by coursework only. Professor Wang's course in e-commerce runs in both the autumn and the spring, and is for more experienced students.

3.15 Relative Pronouns

1a   where

1b   who

1c   which/that

1d   whose

2a   which/that

2b   where

2c   who

2d   which/that

2e   who

2f   which

4a   D

4b   D

4c   A

4d   A

4e   D

5   (Sample answers)

5a   The main campus, which used to be a golf course,

5b   The River Nile, the longest in Africa,

5c   Moscow, the ancient capital of Russia,

5d   Nelson Mandela, who became president of South Africa,

5e   Apples, a fruit associated with many legends,

6a   necessary

6b   not

6c   not

6d   necessary

6e   not

7a   whose

7b   who

7c   which/that

7d   which/that

7e   X

7f   which

7g   whose

7h   which

7i   X

3.16 Singular/Plural

1a   disadvantages – e

1b   are – a

1c   areas – c

1d   crime – b

1e   town has its own council – d

3a   those problems

3b   varies

3c   cultures

3d   are

3e   a job/jobs

3f   A huge/Huge numbers

3g   has

3h   other places

3i   is

3j   lives

4   companies have/websites/e-commerce/this is/businesses/their/trouble/security/expense/ mean/these companies

3.17 Time Words and Phrases

3a   Last

3b   During

3c   By

3d   for

3e   ago

3f   until

3g   Currently

4a   recently

4b   until

4c   for

4d   Last month

4e   by

4f   Since

4g   During

5a   During

5b   Since

5c   ago

5d   recently

5e   Currently

5f   by

5g   since

6a   before

6b   later

6c   by

6d   for

6e   until

6f   during

6g   ago

3.18   Verbs – Formality

2   (Possible synonyms)

adapt = modify

arise = occur

carry out = conduct

characterise = have features of

clarify = explain

concentrate on = look at closely

concern with = deal with

demonstrate = show

determine = find

discriminate = distinguish

emphasise = highlight

establish = lay down/found

exhibit = show

focus on = look at closely

generate = create

hold = be true

identify = pick out

imply = suggest

indicate = show

interact = work together

interpret = explain

manifest = show

overcome = get over

predict = forecast

propose = suggest

prove = turn out

recognise = accept

relate to = link to

supplement = add to

undergo = experience

yield = produce

2a yielded

2b arose

2c demonstrate

2d held

2e emphasised

2f exhibited

2g concerned

2h carried out

3a demonstrate

3b clarify

3c recognised

3d discriminate

3e focus on

3f interpreted

3g overcome

3h   predict

3.19 Verbs – Modal

(Others may be possible throughout this unit)

2a   can

2b   could

2c   cannot

2d   may/can

2e   could

3a   would

3b   might/may/could

3c   could/might/may

3d   should/will/might

3e   will

3f   should/will

3g   could not

4a   should

4b   must

4c   must

4d   should

5a   would (conditional)
     should (suggestion)

5b   may (possibility)
     could (ability)

5c   will (prediction)
     would (conditional)

5d   must (obligation)
     should (suggestion)

5e   may (possibility)
     could (ability)

5f   should (strong possibility)
     may (possibility)

3.20 Verbs – Passives

2a The data were collected and the two groups (were) compared.

2b 120 people in three social classes were interviewed.

2c The results were checked and several errors (were) found.

2d An analysis of the findings will be made.

3a The company was efficiently run by the Connors family until 1981.

3b The house was conveniently built near the station.

3c The portrait of the old man was brilliantly painted by Picasso.

3d Pencils for all the students in the exam were helpfully provided.

3e Over 550 people were regularly tested for the disease (by doctors).

3f The percentages were precisely calculated to three decimal places (by researchers).

3g Their business was optimistically called the Universal Trading Company.

4 (Passives)

was worn out

was born

was called

was helped

was taken over

was assisted

5 Not all – *was born* must be passive

Compare some sentences changed into the active, e.g. 'On his death in 1860 his wife took over the business, and soon their 10-year-old son Jesse assisted her.' This reads rather clumsily compared to the original.

6 (Suggested changes – others possible)

they were married – they married

the factories were used to make – the factories made

Boots was sold – he sold Boots

Boots was bought by a British group – a British group bought Boots

sugar was produced – the factories produced

3.21 Verbs and Prepositions

2a focused on/concentrated on

2b pointed out

2c specialising in

2d   associated with

2e   divided into

2f   blamed for

2g   believed in

2h   rely on

4a   derives from

4b   consists of

4c   added to

4d   looked into

4e   rely on/depend on

4f   invested . . . in

4g   Compared to

4h   pay . . . for

4i   rely on/depend on

3.22 Verbs of Reference

(Others may be possible)

3a   A admitted/accepted/agreed that he might have made a mistake in his estimate.

3b   B denied saying that sheep were faster than horses.

3c   C stated that whales were very intelligent animals.

3d   D agreed with A's position on cats and dogs.

3e   E assumed that cows could get cold in winter.

3f   F concluded that pigs could not fly.

3g   G discovered a new type of frog in the jungle.

3h   H doubted that cats could learn to talk.

3i   I suggested that cat and mouse behaviour should be compared.

3j   J hypothesised that there might be a link between health and the seasons.

5a   L criticised her for being careless about her research methods.

5b   M classified bees into three main species.

5c   N characterised the cat family as the kings of the animal world.

5d   O interpreted dogs' barking as nervousness.

5e   P described trying to estimate the number of animal species as being like shooting in the dark.

5f Q commended/evaluated Darwin as the greatest naturalist of the nineteenth century.

5g R defined insects as six-legged arthropods.

5h S portrayed Queen Victoria as a short, rather fat, dark-eyed woman.

5i T identified/presented Gregor Mendel as the founder of modern genetics.

3.23 Verbs – Tenses

1

	Tense	Reason for use
a	present simple	general rule
b	present continuous	current situation
c	present perfect	recent event
d	present perfect continuous	recent, with emphasis on action that continues for a long time
e	simple past	finished, with time phrase
f	past continuous	finished, with emphasis on action that continues for a long time
g	past perfect	refers to a previous past period
h	future	prediction

2a has been rising/has risen

2b stands for

2c recorded

2d had written

2e will be

2f is considering

2g was building/had built

2h disputes/disputed

2i has fallen/has been falling

4a is/are working

4b believes

4c is looking for

4d is researching

4e   has risen

4f   owns

4g   live

4h   is attending

6a   have suspected

6b   have developed

6c   confirmed

6d   developed

6e   was displayed

6f   demonstrated

6g   says/said

6h   is being tested

6i   makes

6j   developed

6k   will be available

Part 4 – Writing Models

4.1   Formal Letters

1a   Address of sender

1b   Address of recipient

1c   Sender's reference

1d   Date

1e   Greetings

1f   Subject headline

1g   Reason for writing

1h   Further details

1i   Request for response

1j   Ending

1k   Signature

1l   Writer's name and title

2   Model answer

---

54 Sydney Road
Rowborough RB1 6FD

Mr M Bramble
Administrative Assistant
Arts & Social Sciences Admissions Office
Wye House
Central Campus
University of Borchester
Borchester BR3 5HT

Yr Ref: MB/373

5 May 2006

Dear Mr Bramble

Informal Interview

Thank you for inviting me to interview on May 21st. I will be able to attend on that date, but it would be much more convenient if I could have the interview at 12, due to the train times from Rowborough.

Could you please let me know if this alteration is possible?

Yours sincerely

P. Tan

P. Tan

---

3   Model answer

---

54 Sydney Road
Rowborough RB1 6FD

Tel: 0122-354-751

The Manager
Hotel Nelson
Queen's Road
Rowborough RB2 4RN

Yr Ref: EN2

16 October 2006

Dear Sir

Vacancy for Reception Staff

I am writing in response to your advert for reception staff (*Evening News* 15/10).

I am currently studying at Rowborough University, but I am looking for part-time work, and believe that I have the qualities you are seeking. As you will see from my enclosed CV I have previous experience of working in a team, and speak Mandarin and Japanese as well as English. Having no family commitments I am quite prepared to work evenings or weekends.

I believe that I could make a useful contribution to your business, which I am considering as a future career, and hope to hear from you soon.

Yours faithfully

P. Tan

P. Tan

Enc. CV

4.3   Reporting and Designing Surveys

1   (Other suggestions possible/in any order)

Get up-to-date data

Collect information about the behaviour of a specific group, e.g. overseas students in London

Check/replicate other research

2a   conducted

2b   random

2c   questionnaire

2d   questioned

2e   respondents

2f   Interviewees

2g   mentioned

2h   majority

2i   slightly

2j   minority

2k   questions

2l   common

2m   generally

2n   sample

3   Model questions. (3–6 could use present tense)

Q2   Why did you take a job?

Q3   What effect did the work have on your studies?

Q4   What kind of work did you do?

Q5   What hours did you work?

Q6   How much did you earn?

Q7   Do you have any comments on your work?

4a   past tense

4b   present tense

The survey is completed but the results are still valid.

5   (ii) is less embarrassing for most people to answer.

6   (i) is an open question and has many possible answers.

(ii) is a closed question with a limited range of responses.

7   For casual interviews ten is probably the maximum most interviewees will cope with.

4.5   Comparison Essay

(Other answers possible)

a   It normally involves having access to a secure site on the internet where a graded series of lessons are available, and which have assignments sent and returned by email.

b   A student living in a small town in China, for example, can now study a course at an American college.

c   Membership of a group may also create a useful spirit of competition, which stimulates learning.

d   There may be many people who are unable, either through work or family commitments, or due to lack of funds, to go to classes . . .

e   Although on-line courses are now offered by many institutions . . .

f   . . . it is by no means clear that they offer real advantages compared to classroom education.

g   e-education/on-line courses/internet use in education/e-learning

4.6   Discussion Essay

1

1   F

2   C

3   A

4   G

5   E

6   B

7   D

2

Addition	Result	Reason	Time	Example	Opposition
while	so that	since	first	e.g.	but
and	therefore	due to	then	for example	yet
as well as		because of		such as	however
also				for instance	

WRITING TESTS

Writing Test 1

Note that in some cases, e.g. (1a), only one answer is acceptable; in other cases, e.g. (1b), a number of synonyms are possible, not all of which may be listed.

1a   in

1b   problem/difficulty/challenge/priority

1c   the/so

1d   difficult/problematic/challenging

1e   However/Next/Then

1f   or

1g   improves

1h   begins/tends/seems

1i   in/after

1j   they

1k   easily/well/effectively

1l   third/further

1m most

1n   since/because/as

1o   on

1p   why

1q   necessary/better/useful/helpful

1r   an

1s   before

1t   their

Writing Test 2

Speaking and Writing

1)   When we speak, it is normally to one or

2)   a small number of people, who are often well known to us.

3)   As we speak, we are able

4)   to study our listeners' faces for expressions which tell

5)   us their reaction to what we are saying;

6)   for example agreement, or amusement.

7)   If their expressions show incomprehension

8)   we will probably restate what we are saying.

9)   For most people speaking feels like a natural activity,

10) though if they have to make a formal speech

11) they often find the situation stressful.

1)   Writing, however, is much more like speaking to

2)   an unknown audience.

3)   Unless we are writing a letter to a friend

4)   we have no way of knowing who may read our words.

5)   Writers cannot check if the readers understand, or are interested

6)   in what they are writing.

7)   This is the reason why writing is more difficult than

8)   speaking, and often uses a more formal style.

9)   It also explains why writing must be as clear and simple as possible,

10) to avoid the dangers of being misunderstood by readers

11) who cannot look puzzled to

12) make the writer explain what he means again.

Writing Test 3

Note comments in Writing Test 1 above.

3a   somewhere

3b   from

3c   who

3d   kinds/types/sorts/categories

3e   Almost/Nearly/Virtually

3f   halls

3g   make/find

3h   convenient/practical/sensible

3i   but/although/though

3j   rather

3k   a

3l   This

3m   may/might/can/could/should

3n   also

3o   on

3p   as/since/because

3q   be

3r   vital/important/essential/critical

3s   an

3t   them

Writing Test 4

Model answer

A COMPARISON OF BORCHESTER AND ROWBOROUGH AS A STUDY LOCATION

Rowborough is a large industrial city with a population of one and a half million, while Borchester is an old city with a much smaller population. These basic differences determine their suitability as centres for a university course.

Rowborough can offer a wider range of leisure facilities but Borchester has a quieter character. Rowborough may have a worse climate, being cool even in summer and wet in winter, while winters in Borchester are less cold, though the summers tend to be wet.

Rowborough is hillier than Borchester, which might be a drawback for cyclists. However, Rowborough does have a better public transport system, which may compensate for the hills. Borchester also has a rather remote campus, which might involve a lot of travelling. It is also likely to be more expensive in terms of accommodation, and is rather distant from the capital. On the other hand, some areas in Rowborough suffer from high crime rates.

Clearly, each city has its advantages: Borchester is more likely to suit a student looking for peace and quiet, who can tolerate some inconvenience, while Rowborough would be suitable for someone keen to economise and wanting a more lively atmosphere.

Sources

Quotations from the following articles will be found in various units. As the quotations have been made to give examples of language, rather than for reasons of content, in-text references are not made.

Ardila, A. 2001. Predictors of university academic performance in Colombia. *International Journal of Educational Research* 35 (4) 411–17

Bardet, J.-P. 2001. Early marriage in pre-modern France. *The History of the Family* 6 (3) 345–63

Benoit, D., Madigan, S., Lecce, S., Shea, B. and Goldberg, S. 2001. Atypical maternal behaviour toward feeding-disordered infants before and after intervention. *Infant Mental Health Journal* 22 (6) 611–26

Chakrabarti, S. and Chakrabarti, S. Rural electrification programme with solar energy in remote region – a case study in an island. *Energy Policy* 30 (1) 33–42

Creeber, G. 2001. 'Taking our personal lives seriously': intimacy, continuity and memory in the television serial. *Media, Culture & Society* 23 439–55

Davis, G. 2002. Is the claim that 'variance kills' an ecological fallacy? *Accident Analysis and Prevention* 34 (3) 343–6

Dündar, Ö. 2001. Models of urban transformation. Informal housing in Ankara. *Cities* 18 (6) 391–401

Grant, J., Meller, W., and Urevig, B. 2001. Changes in psychiatric consultations over ten years. *General Hospital Psychiatry* 23 (5) 261–5

Hendry, E. 2001. Masonry walls: materials and constructions. *Construction and Building Materials* 15 (8) 323–30

Horton, E., Folland, C. and Parker, D. 2001. The changing incidence of extremes in worldwide and central England temperatures to the end of the twentieth century. *Climatic Change* 50 267–95

Job, N., van Exel, A. and Rietveld, P. 2001. Public transport strikes and traveller behaviour. *Transport Policy* 8 (4) 237–46

Kinder, T. 2001. The use of call centres by local public administrations. *Futures* 33 (10) 837–60

Marxsen, C. 2001. Potential world garbage and waste carbon sequestration. *Environmental Science & Policy* 4 (6) 293–300

Nazarov, V., Radostin, A. and Stepanyants, Y. 2001. Influence of water content in river sand on the self-brightening of acoustic waves. *Applied Acoustics* 62 (12) 1347–58

O'Sullivan, D. 2002. Framework for managing business development in the networked organisation. *Computers in Industry* 47 (1) 77–88

Otero, J. and Milas, C. 2001. Modelling the spot prices of various coffee types. *Economic Modelling* 18 (4) 625–41

Pogrebin, M. and Dodge, M. 2001. Women's accounts of their prison experiences. A retrospective view of their subjective realities. *Journal of Criminal Justice* 29 (6) 531–41

Sánchez-Moreno, E. 2001. Cross-cultural links in ancient Iberia: socio-economic anatomy of hospitality. *Oxford Journal of Archaeology* 20 (4) 391–414

Selmer, J. 2001. Coping and adjustment of Western expatriate managers in Hong Kong. *Scandinavian Journal of Management* 17 (2) 167–85

Semple, J. 2000. Production of transgenic rice with agronomically useful genes. *Biotechnology Advances* 18 (8) 653–83

Smith, L. and Haddad, L. 2001. How important is improving food availability for reducing child nutrition in developing countries? *Agricultural Economics* 26 (3) 191–204

Tedesco, L. 2000. La ñata contra el vidrio: urban violence and democratic governability in Argentina. *Bulletin of Latin American Research* 19 (4) 527–45

Worthington, R. 2001. Between Hermes and Themis: an empirical study of the contemporary judiciary in Singapore. *Journal of Law & Society* 28 (4) 490–519